One Foot in Front of the Other

The Journey of a Million Steps

Mike Duhacek

One Foot in Front of the Other
Copyright © 2020 by Mike Duhacek

About Author Picture – Ian MacAlpine, The Whig-Standard
Pictures of the walk – Joe Girodat, Nicole Girodat, Ed Crocket

All rights reserved. No part of this publication may be reproduced, distributed, or transmitted in any form or by any means, including photocopying, recording, or other electronic or mechanical methods, without the prior written permission of the author, except in the case of brief quotations embodied in critical reviews and certain other non-commercial uses permitted by copyright law.

Tellwell Talent
www.tellwell.ca

ISBN
978-0-2288-3744-2 (Hardcover)
978-0-2288-3745-9 (Paperback)

Dedication

This book is dedicated to the entire HMBC team and especially to my mom, who was the one that taught me how to put one foot in front of the other.

A portion of the proceeds from this book will be donated to the Canadian Cancer Society.

Introduction

My sister, Nicole, and I were always close to our mom growing up. Our bond became even closer when my parents separated. I was 14, and my sister, 16. My mom was 35. We moved from a house to an apartment with two bedrooms, and supported each other through the transition. My mom insisted my sister and I would each have our own bedroom, to have our own space. She said she would buy a good pull out couch and sleep in the living room, because as long as we were together under the same roof, that was all that mattered to her. I truly believed her, because my mom's number one thing in life, was Nicole and I. The three of us were a happy family while we lived in our apartment.

About five years later, my mom re-married an amazing man, Ed. A few years later, my sister also married an incredible guy, Joey. Soon after, I married the most beautiful girl I have ever seen, who is now my wonderful wife, Erin. Jumping ahead, my sister and her husband now have three beautiful children, and Erin and I have two perfect boys. Since the event happened that is the reason for this book, we added a beautiful addition to our family, our precious little girl. We are now a close family of twelve.

Growing up, and through our adult life, Nicole and I were always very close to our grandparents on my mother's side. To this day I have wonderful memories of moments and events that we shared, such as holidays, as well as the simple every day kind. I not only got a kick out of them, I learned from them, and respected, enjoyed and loved them. They were always there for us, and always welcomed me with open arms when I showed up to their house unannounced for a visit. I grew up a short distance from their house, which made it possible to visit a few times a week. They loved their family and each other very much. They were known to family and friends as our "Nan and Ba," a nickname from our childhood that stuck.

My Nan and Ba were both diagnosed, and lost their battle with cancer, in a very short time. It was hard on my whole family, to lose them both in a difficult way within 16 months, even though I know that many families go through the same thing. Frankly, I felt anger that cancer took both of them. I think it took a lot out of my mom. She was always there for them, day in and day out, throughout their journey. She did whatever she could to see her parents got everything they needed. Although, this was not surprising to me, as that's just the way my mom is. She loves her family with all her heart, and would do anything for any one of us.

Shortly after losing her parents, my mom was diagnosed, at 54, with a rare, late stage three or early stage four, cancer. It came as a complete shock and devastated all of us. In her own words, she wrote on the helpmeburycancer website, "In the spring of 2010, at fifty-four years of age, I knew I was tired, but I chalked it up to fatigue. I had lost my mom to non-hodgkins lymphoma in October 2008 and my dad to lung cancer in February 2010, but I never thought it would hit me. I began having intermittent pain in my right side and thought maybe I'd pulled something packing up my dad's things. I went to my family doctor and during examination he asked me if I hadn't felt the lump in my right side. Lump? He wrote urgent on an ultrasound form and my journey into the unknown began.

As I waited in the dark while they did the ultrasound, I knew this was big. I wished I had brought someone in my family. I had no idea how much I would come to need my family in the next two and a half years. The first specialist my husband and I met with was blunt. You have stage three cancer, possibly early stage four. It was a moment that will be forever etched in my mind. She left the room. My husband put his arms around me while I just repeated "Jesus Christ" over and over. A deep fear set in, indescribable to those who haven't heard those words before.

We went home and the love of my family surrounded me. I had lost both of my parents to cancer in the past year and a half, and although I loved them dearly, I thanked God they weren't still around to hear this about their only daughter.

My daughter, son, brother and sister-in-law got on their computers and researched my cancer like my life depended on it, which of course, it did. We knew we needed to find a surgeon who saw me as a person as well as a patient, who could give me a glimmer of hope.

My sister-in-law suggested my current surgeon at the Juravinski Cancer Centre in Hamilton, Ontario. He has travelled this journey with me and I count him among my blessings. He and his team at the Juravinski are not only brilliant doctors, but they are kind and respectful as well.

I had my first surgery to remove my tumour in July 2010. When I woke up my beloved children and husband surrounded me. They told me I still had the tumour inside me, that the doctors had decided they needed to do chemo and radiation first. I cried.

I started concurrent chemo and radiation in August 2010. By the end of September 2010, I was admitted to the hospital, weak and dehydrated. The night before my last radiation and chemo treatment, I was taken to emergency with an extremely high heart rate. Once again, my children magically appeared, which was becoming a habit. They vowed to be with me every step of the way.

In October I rested at home waiting for my November surgery. I was so weak I had begun to whisper, as talking took too much effort. I had a blood transfusion at that time, as my hemoglobin was far too low.

Finally, November 4, 2010 arrived and I had my second surgery, which lasted almost eight hours. My tumour was large, and had completely taken over my appendix. They did a right hemicolectomy, and took out most of my psoas muscle, leaving me with a permanent leg disability. I woke up in intensive care hallucinating. It was the worst night of my life.

After sixteen days in the hospital, I couldn't get my own leg in and out of the bed and had to use a walker. I went home a changed woman. I began physiotherapy immediately, but it was hampered at first as I was still vomiting so much. I was advised to do more chemo in February, but after a couple of sessions I had to stop. My weight was down almost forty pounds, and I could keep nothing in me.

I continued with physio when I could, although I knew I would eventually hit a wall, as a major muscle had been cut, as well as others, and could not be rehabilitated. In May of that year, my leg was numb and I didn't feel it hit something. I fell hard and ended up in emergency again. It put my physio back by months.

In April I faced the dreaded day that all cancer patients fear. I was diagnosed with a recurrence. My daughter was with me when my oncologist told me they had found a new 'spot'. They were going to schedule more chemo. The second my daughter and I stepped on the elevator after leaving the doctor's office, we looked at each other. The doors closed and we hugged on the way down. My husband came home from work immediately and my children both stayed with us. I told them that if this was it for me, to always remember to look the other way when they missed me. By that I meant that I wanted them to look at the beautiful, precious generation coming up behind them, so full of life.

I began a 'cocktail' of chemo, different this time from the ones I had tried before. In May, my hair began to fall out in clumps, until you could see my scalp. By June, I was so weak five days after my infusion I had to measure whether it was worth the effort to pick up the phone or TV remote. By the end of that month my oncologist stopped the chemo as my cancer wasn't responding. My 'spot' had gotten bigger.

In October 2012, I had my third surgery, again lasting about eight hours. Once again, my husband and children were there. This time the surgeon removed my kidney, my gallbladder, part of my duodenum, more of my psoas muscle and three different areas of intestines. I woke up with my family surrounding me. The only thing I remember is my children kissing me and saying they loved me. I tried to joke with them so they'd know I was okay, but my words just came out jumbled.

I was in the hospital twelve days, and then home for nine more, when I developed a fever. My husband took me to emergency where an infection was diagnosed. Another few days in the hospital."

I'll never forget the feeling I had sitting in the hospital watching my mom being so brave, but knowing that she was struggling, particularly when she was in pain. Sitting in the waiting room watching so many other families around me go through similar scenarios, while they waited for a loved one that was in surgery, or receiving treatment. Of course, we all waited outside the operating room for all of her surgeries. But the memory that is the clearest, is the memory of going outside, and looking up at a sign on the side of the hospital wall. It stated that one in three Canadians will be diagnosed with cancer in their lifetime. I stood staring at that sign. I remember the feeling of frustration that poured through my body that day. My grandparents, all the people in this hospital, one in three Canadians and now, my beloved mother, was inside fighting for her life.

Driving home that day, I wished cancer was visible and something tangible that I could grab onto. I wanted to shake it, hit it, drag it around and make it suffer like it does to so many people. I got home that night and spoke to my wife about how I felt. Erin, always supportive, listened to me replay my day and explain the deep frustration I felt. I knew it was time to start thinking about what I could do, what role I could play in raising awareness and funds, to fight this disease. I said I needed to do something, something big. She fully understood how serious I was, but was anxious to hear the extent of my thoughts. I told her I wanted to fight back against cancer. Her expression was proud, yet her concern was evident.

I said I felt anger watching my mom in so much pain. I looked at Erin and said, 'What does cancer look like? What could I drag behind me, if I do a walk, that depicts cancer?' Erin asked where and when I was going to do this. I told her I wanted to go a far distance and wanted to do it in the winter, so that whatever object I chose to depict cancer would be punished, while I dragged it behind me. So that I would be tested too, just like people who have cancer are tested. Like their family members are tested.

Erin's eyes were locked on me as ideas started pouring out of me. Ontario. I want to pull cancer across the entire province. I want to do this for my mom and anyone else that is dealing with this disease. In my own small way, I want to symbolize the weight and burden that it is, to drag this weight around with you, day in and day out. To show cancer patients and their families my sincere respect.

Erin had her own questions. How long will this take you? How much will the load you're dragging weigh? Where will you sleep? How far can you go every day? How long will you have to train for this? I absorbed all of the helpful questions and stared out the window, asking myself if I could do it. I turned to her and said, "We'll have to think of all these things and make a list." She asked me if I was serious, and after I said yes, she hugged me tightly. I knew how supportive she was of both me and this idea, but I also knew she was worried and protective. She said she was so proud of me, what an amazing cause it was, but at the same time she knew it would take a toll on my body.

The next morning, we decided that I should go see my mom to see how she was and to see if we could do anything for her. She was still just weeks out of her third major surgery. We both agreed that if there's a time to tell her my thoughts, it's now. I'll never forget the look on my mom's face when I told her. It took a moment for it to sink in. The announcement was unexpected, to say the least. I told her I was going to drag something that looked like cancer across Ontario to raise awareness and funds. Do something to turn my negative energy into something positive. My mom asked with who, and thought I meant on a team. I told her it would be just me. My step-dad, Ed, came into the room wondering what he had missed. My mom told him that I wanted to walk across Ontario. "What?" Ed said. "Do you know how far that is?" I smiled and said, "Far". They looked at each other, and then me. My mom's eyes were filled up and she said she was overwhelmed with pride. She said she would do whatever I needed her to do, that she knew my sister would be all over this, too. She asked when I was going to do this. I said, next winter. She looked at me and said that she sure hoped she was here to see it.

The phone rang after I arrived home. It was my mom, asking if I would consider doing it this February, instead of a year from now. I didn't learn until later that it was because she wanted to make sure she would be able to witness it, and didn't know what her future would hold. When I got off the phone, Erin and I talked about the timing of this walk and decided that the walk wasn't going to wait for a year. We needed to assemble our team and plan for it now. I wanted my mom to see it as much as she wanted to see me do it.

It was discussed with my sister and her family, extended family, my in-laws and colleagues at work. Their reactions were all different but all very supportive. My family immediately started to lay out what needed to be done. Each quickly claimed responsibility for tasks that would need to be planned, organized and worked on in the next couple of months. We were going to have to hustle. It became a well-oiled machine that worked every single day, with an overwhelming never-ending workload of things to do.

We brainstormed what I could pull, what this initiative would be called, logistics of the trip and how this would all be funded. Other topics included what I would eat, where I would sleep and how I would prepare for this very gruelling journey. The checklist started with creating a website, both Facebook and Twitter accounts, a training schedule, what I was going to pull, when I was going to do this, and who to notify.

Our team brainstormed and bounced ideas off each other constantly. I said I wanted to drag something that depicted cancer, wanting it to be as heavy as I could handle, and be something that wouldn't damage the roads. Someone asked what I was going to do with the 'cancer' when I was done pulling it. I thought about it and said, bury it. Put it in the ground where it belongs. The entire team agreed that there was nothing better to depict cancer than the actual word itself. A big, heavy and bright word that everyone could read as I walked along. The sliding or dragging characteristics were the next topic for discussion. What could be more Canadian than pulling this word on a sled? Ed spoke up and said he could build it. He would paint the letters on the sled bright canary yellow, so it couldn't be missed. It was that evening that 'Help Me Bury Cancer' was born.

Preparation

The next week I went to my brother-in-law Joey's family farm. I picked out a heavy, rustic, 75 pound barn beam, attached some pull chains to it and used that to prepare my body for the walk. I chose long country roads, as well as thick mud and gravel that would simulate snow, and pulled this weight for hours at a time, day in and day out. I got a lot of sideways looks when I pulled it around town. It was exhausting, but necessary. Ed built the cancer letters and sled during the months of my training. My sister contacted the Canadian Cancer Society and told them what was being planned. They were enthusiastic and said it was a dream to have something like this outside of their planned events. We were so happy to be able to do this and donate any funds to them. We told them we wouldn't use any money donated from this walk to cover expenses, that if we couldn't get sponsors our family would fund ourselves.

As my mom was quickly preparing press releases, my team and I were now being contacted by the media who was supportive in getting the word out. As soon as I could, I started pulling the completed sled and letters around town. Those sideways looks turned to questions, honks and cheers from the residents of my town, Milton. On those training nights, I started to receive the first donations. People stopped their cars to watch me, or came out on their porch when I passed by, to say, "Go Mike, go." The website and all our social media pages were now live, with growing hits to them daily. The Canadian Cancer Society was organizing events and speaking functions to help broadcast the message of this upcoming mission.

I was so fortunate to be selected to drop the puck at the Oakville Blades, Pink in the Rink hockey game. This is a prestigious annual event put on by the Cancer Society, to support breast cancer, and I was honoured to be a part of it. I was able to pull my sled out onto the ice before the game, while the master of ceremonies broadcasted the Help Me Bury Cancer story to the spectators. I also appreciated having some great interviews that night, that would help with publicity.

My team was busy planning the walk route, updating the social media pages, seeking sponsors, making meal plans, finding a burial site for the cancer letters and locating a motorhome, which would act as our support vehicle to drive behind me across the province. My employer and second family, the Halton Regional Police, were also busy doing whatever they could to support me, which included a few employees giving me generous amounts of food and gas cards, my department organizing an amazing fundraiser lunch and the Service assisting with contacting fellow police agencies along my route. I was so grateful and will never forget their overwhelming support, generosity, and willingness to help.

As I continued to train, it was getting colder outside. It was time to select a starting date. I chose February 4, 2013, so I could do my estimated month-long journey through the roughest winter month. It would be a way to symbolize, in some small way, what cancer patients and their families go though. This was also a special date as it is World Cancer Day. My mom immediately started to look into possible starting points in the City of Windsor. February was fast approaching. It really began to sink in when I turned on the radio and heard the popular radio show, Derringer in the morning on Q107, talking about our mission. What amazing exposure!

I found myself staring at my website countdown counter watching every second tick off, knowing the start date was right around the corner. A rush of adrenaline went through me. I felt ready, I felt anxious. I felt strong. I felt like nothing could stand in my way of me reaching my goal. Not snow, or cold, or exhaustion, would come between me and my ultimate destination. But most of all, as I sat there, I could feel every one of my supporters and their unwavering support behind me.

My mom had arranged for columnist Jeff Mahoney of the Hamilton Spectator newspaper to interview us at her house. Jeff was empathetic, supportive, and we couldn't have asked for a better column. The morning it came out we received a lovely comment from someone who worked for the City of Hamilton, saying that he had lost his mom to cancer, and to let him know if he could help. I believe his name was Mike, too, if memory serves me correctly. A few more interviews were lined up directly after that, including a great interview with Julie Slack of the Milton Champion newspaper.

Someone told me I was being billed as a 'regular Canadian guy', like they were unsure of my reaction. I smiled. Let me tell you, that's one of the best compliments I could ever get. I'm seventh or eighth generation Canadian on my mom's side. Love my hot drink at Tim Horton's. Nothing better to me than the sound of a hockey stick hitting a puck on a crisp winter day. I was about to walk across a safe province, in a safe country, with my fellow Canadians cheering me on, and supporting me. Determined, hardworking, regular Canadians, just like me who really believe that together, we can make a difference.

February 3, 2013 arrived, the day before the start of the walk. The motorhome was sitting in my mom and Ed's driveway and I was packing my outerwear that Columbia and Canada Goose had donated. Next, I adjusted my custom-made pulling harness that had been shipped from Australia. The people who made it put a note with it, saying, "You'll fly". The sled was ready for any kind of weather that February could throw at me. We always planned for the sled to weigh about 110 lbs,

Mike Duhacek

but the actual finished weight was 125 lbs. My team thought that was a lot for a 900 km journey, but I decided to do it.

Driving the few hours to Windsor, I felt like we would never arrive. My son kept asking if I was going to walk all the way back. I said, "Sure am buddy," nonchalantly, while my stomach had butterflies. When we pulled into Windsor they welcomed us with open arms. My mom had arranged radio interviews for me, which included AM800, a wonderful interview and photoshoot with the Windsor Star newspaper and a fabulous interview with CTV News. She had also contacted the Holiday Inn on Huron Church Street to say we were coming, and they generously donated rooms to us. It was obvious that Windsor wanted to help me bury cancer.

I remember lying in bed at 3:30 a.m., February 4, 2013, wide awake, again with butterflies in my stomach. Within hours I would be outside on a cold, crisp winter day, strapping on a 125 lb sled to my back, and taking my first of over 1,000,000 steps no matter what the weather, to achieve my goal of walking across the province of Ontario in the month of February. I was beginning in Windsor and would end in Ottawa. It was an intimidating thought.

I would never allow myself to think I couldn't do it. I constantly repeated, "You've got this. Focus. You've got this. Focus!" I knew I needed to do this for myself, my family, friends, every cancer patient who couldn't do it, and their family members, who were suffering just like ours. The media was now behind me, broadcasting to whoever was listening, that a man was beginning his trek from Windsor, to bury cancer in Ottawa, on Monday February 4, 2013 at 7:00 a.m. I was committed. I was determined to make a difference, determined to raise awareness and show compassion to my fellow Canadians that were fighting this disease. This was much bigger than me now.

Day 1

We pulled into the dimly lit parking lot where I would begin, at 6:45 a.m. To this day, I don't remember the ride from the hotel to our designated starting point. My mind was filled with thoughts of how it might go, how it might feel, how my body would react. My family surrounded me when I stepped out of the support vehicle, including my wife and our two children, my sister, her husband and their three children, and my mom and step-dad. The five kids, Jesse, Jace, Jaiden, Emma and Dylan lined up, holding a banner to cheer me on. Three Windsor police cruisers pulled up at 6:55 a.m. These officers would escort me through Windsor making sure the start of my mission, was a safe one. I hugged and kissed my family goodbye. We took pictures and suddenly, it was time. I walked up behind the cruisers as they activated their lights. A Windsor officer looked at me and said, "You tell us when you're ready." I took a deep breath and ensured that my sled was properly fastened to my harness. I looked up at the sky and mouthed, "Give me the strength to do this," clapped my hands together and yelled, "Let's do it!" The first cruiser pulled out to block traffic, the second led the way for me, while the third tucked behind me as I started my sled pull. The energy I felt was something that I have never experienced. My family and I had spoken about conserving energy on the first day, and how my adrenalin would carry me faster than my standard pace. It did exactly that. I rushed out of that Windsor parking lot like I was in a sprint.

When we started walking down the city streets it was rush hour on a Monday morning. This was part of the plan. We knew that we would be looking at getting as much attention as possible and starting at morning commute was doing just that. Cars started to honk, in acknowledgement. Windows were rolled down in cars, with screams of, "Go Mike, go" echoing from them. People were coming out onto their front porches, clapping and cheering. Cars were stopping, with people getting out and donating to my cause, in the middle of the road. I had people starting to walk with me, giving me encouragement, telling me I can do it, and they would be following me.

I cannot tell you the feeling I had, to know that my fellow Ontarian's were supporting me with every step I took, supporting this cause that touches almost all of us. I radioed back to my support vehicle and told Ed and Joey that I felt great, and that this was incredible. When we approached another intersection, the light turned yellow. The cruisers stopped in the middle of the intersection and blocked traffic while our entire entourage got through safely. All across the province, police kept not only me safe, but ensured the safety of the public as well.

We turned the next corner and what an amazing sight lay ahead. The Windsor Police Headquarters staff lined the street and supported me with cheers, yelling, "You can do this! Go Mike, go!" To have the support from a fellow police department was incredible and emotional, all at the same time. I felt a huge boost of motivation as I felt that the entire city of Windsor completely were on our team. I put my head down and kept going. As I was going down a hill, CBC news was filming every step I took. I kept thinking to myself, are they here for me? It was hard for me to wrap my head around. My eyes focused on the road ahead. I could make out someone that was crossing the street in the distance. Then, another. As my eyes continued to focus, I thought I saw a lot of people on both sides of the road. I couldn't tell if it was people or trees lining the roads, as it was still too far away. I radioed back to my support vehicle and asked what they saw ahead. Ed and Joey responded, and said it looked like a lot of people. I said, I think the same thing, but couldn't comprehend that it could be for us. As I pulled my sled closer to them, it became very obvious. The streets were lined with students from a high school. They were all waiting for us. Students and staff on both sides of the street cheering at the top of their lungs, displaying their hand made signs of encouragement. St. Joseph's

One Foot in Front of the Other

High School were lighting it up. I radioed back to Ed and Joey and said, "Wow!" Walking through the high school crowd, giving them high fives and feeling everyone supporting me, was simply awesome. Kids ran from the other side of the street to shake my hand or pat me on the back. A younger generation, totally connected to this mission, how cool was that? Once I passed the entire group I looked back, and put my hands over my head to applaud them for braving the cold to support me. People wonder when they do a rally like this if it helps, and I'm here to tell you that it absolutely does.

I put my head down, as I now had a minute to reflect on what had just happened. As the thoughts and images were going through my head, my feet were starting to burn, noticeable in almost every step I took. Looking ahead again, now I could see the Tucumseh Ontario Provincial Police waiting for me. I knew that this was the end of the line for my amazing Windsor Police escort. I stopped and shook the three officer's hands. They were with me the whole way through their jurisdiction. I told them that I would never forget their support, and to please follow my journey on the helpmeburycancer website all the way to Ottawa. They smiled and said it was their pleasure and that they would without a doubt, be following me. Wishing me the best of luck, they said the Ontario Provincial Police would take it from there. I introduced myself to the O.P.P officer and enthusiastically, she said she was proud to lead the way for me. She asked if she should be doing anything special, such as a specific speed or positioning of the cruiser. I smiled and told her as long as you lead the way for me, I'd be fine with tucking in behind the cruiser and focusing on the bumper for a while.

Snow was falling, and once it settled on the ground it was really starting to make the sled drag. I could feel that my legs were tired and my feet were still burning. Ed and Joey radioed up to me and said to take a break. Maybe I needed food, or needed to rest my body for ten minutes. I saw a park on the right side of the road and pointed to the lot until I got the officer's attention. She pulled her cruiser in as I followed with my sled. The support vehicle coasted in behind me. The officer got out of her vehicle and said I was doing great. She said that my form was starting to change. Ed and Joey agreed. To be honest, I knew that was the case as well. However, I said that I didn't feel great, as I walked inside the motor home to repack my feedbag with as many carbs as my body could handle. I also had a quick second lunch and a bottle of Gatorade hoping that I was just losing a bit of steam. Ed and Joey asked if I was ready, and my answer was yes. It was mid-afternoon and I had been on the road for about 35 kms and I knew that I wanted to get 50 kms behind me the first day. As I continued to pull my sled down a long country road, every second vehicle was giving me supportive honks. Every 15 minutes or so a car would pull over with a donation. This was the motivation I needed to find the strength to take me another 15 kms. Ed and Joey were so supportive, as I knew they would be, asking what I needed, telling me I was doing awesome, and providing me updates of messages of support that were being posted on our Facebook page.

One Foot in Front of the Other

The snow was still falling and a mother and her son came riding up on their bikes to greet me. They said they passed me in their car about thirty minutes ago. When they got home, they jumped on their bikes to come and find out about my venture and to donate at the same time. It was really cool to be standing in the middle of the road, in the middle of the country, in the middle of winter, talking to a mom and her son about why I was doing this. They brought their camera, so Ed and Joey could take a few pictures of us. One of those pictures ended up as a chosen picture for Day One of my blog that night. As I continued, my feet were numb and my knees were sore. I was looking forward to having the first day behind me. I was anxious to put my feet up. Ed radioed up to me and said I walked 50 kms. As much as I wanted to stop right then and there, I said that I wanted to travel one more kilometer to make it 51. I had told myself and everyone else, that 50 kms was my goal. I thought if I went 51, it would be a mental boost, knowing I had exceeded my first day goal.

At 51 kms I stopped. My legs were about to fold. My step-dad unclipped my sled from my harness. My muscles were burning, my arms were weak, my body was chilled and it was the first time that I started to worry about my feet. Every step I took towards the motor home felt like my feet were on fire.

I stepped inside, and Joey tore off my hat, unzipped my coat and started to unlace my boots. While I was sitting on the couch slurping down a protein drink and eating whatever was in sight, my brother-in-law had the first boot off. He slipped the first layered sock off, followed by the other, and turned to Ed and said, "Oh no!" I'll never forget the expression on their faces, even though they were trying to be positive. I wore the wrong socks and doubled them up at the start of the day in fear that my feet would be too cold, as my boots were not insulated. The opposite happened. My feet overheated and blistered badly. I leaned down and started to peel the bottom of my foot off. They were raw. They were on fire. Joey said we needed to take care of these by keeping them clean and to not allow this to happen again. Here it was day one and my feet were jeopardizing the entire walk. I leaned back on the couch and focused my eyes on the ceiling with an absolute sick feeling in my stomach. I thought of all of the preparation, all of the support and realized my stupid mistake regarding footwear, could cost me the success of the walk.

I needed to focus, to start my blog, refuel my body and get some rest. I knew no matter how bad my feet felt, I was going to be back out on the road first thing in the morning. I knew this wasn't the time to start feeling sorry for myself and I believed that there wasn't much else that could stand in the way of me completing my goal.

Ed and Joey were so helpful and supportive that night. Every opportunity they had, they complimented me on how well I did the first day. They got me anything I needed and helped me into bed. They had my back in every way possible.

I called home before going to sleep, to speak with my family to tell them I was okay, and to tell them that I missed them. My wife Erin and our two little guys were so supportive, just as I knew they would be. I also knew that they wanted me to be home with them, but understood I needed to do this. I told them all that I loved them and hung up the phone. I lay in bed wide awake and very cold. As vehicles drove by us on the side of the road, the support vehicle would rock back and forth. That repetitive movement would eventually put me to sleep.

Day 2

The next morning, we woke to dense fog on Tecumseh Road, just outside of Windsor. I laid in bed with a nervous feeling in my stomach, at the thought of what my legs would feel like when I tried to get up. I wondered if my feet were better or worse than the night before. Joey and Ed were already up preparing for a new day. They were busy looking over maps and setting up the sled for another day of slugging. I heard Ed talking to my mom on the phone, saying I was doing okay. I heard that the support counts on my website were growing quickly. The media coverage from TV, radio, newspapers, and word of mouth was increasing, as I had pulled my sled over 50 kms the day before.

I was ready for another full day of meeting new people and spreading cancer awareness. I ate a huge breakfast. I felt like I could have kept eating, but knew I had to suit up and get out there. I started packing my feedbag with enough food and drinks to last me for half a day. I was eating as I walked every hour or so, and doing my best to keep my carbs at their maximum.

Ed, Joey and I spoke about how it might be a good idea to add a morning video to my blog. Just a short 20-60 second video, to let people know where I was, where I was going, and what the weather was like. As I stepped out of the support vehicle, my legs were stiff and my feet felt a bit cold, as I only was wearing one thin layer of socks. I knew my feet would heat up as the day went on. It had taken me about 20 minutes to wrap and bandage my feet, to make sure they were protected the best they could be for the day.

I was only out of the support vehicle a couple of minutes when the first car pulled up to offer some kind words and financial support. The woman said she saw my story on the news and thought I was doing one of the bravest things she'd ever heard of. Of course, I was humbled and said I was just trying to do my part. She said my goal was ambitious and that she would pray for my safe arrival in Ottawa. She shared that she had lost her mom and dad to cancer, and was 100% behind me. It was the exact motivation I needed to last me the entire day. I was walking and pulling the word cancer behind me in full support of people like this. I asked her to please follow my journey, just before she pulled away. She stared at me for about five seconds not saying a word, but with tears falling down her cheeks. As she drove away, I knew she didn't need to say a word for me to know I had her support, the entire way.

I told Ed I was ready to be strapped in. I put my arms up in the air as he fastened the sled to my harness. I took one step forward and could feel the weight. It was nice to be hooked into the sled again, in a funny way. I was mentally preparing myself for another day of pain. Ed started recording my few words, before I started out. Looking ahead all I could see was a long straight country road.

I told Ed and Joey that I was ready as they pulled the motor home in behind me, to protect me from traffic. I turned my ipod to the Rolling Stones and worked my way down the road with my head down as I spoke to my legs. I was asking them to loosen up and to be strong.

Ed and Joey said that the first little town I would be coming to was in about 10 kms, and was called Stoney Point. My short term goal was just to get to this town. I wasn't going to pressure myself and psyche myself out, by thinking too far ahead into the day. This was the first time I realized I had to break apart these long days into smaller, more manageable goals. This would be mentally rewarding and would assist with my confidence level. I knew I had to do whatever it took, every minute of every hour, to succeed.

I reached into my feedbag to grab some food and a drink of Gatorade. My drink was already completely frozen. It was an example of how cold it was and gave me something to concentrate on for a while, trying to get some slush out of the bottle to hydrate. My hands were always hot.

It was very rare that I wore gloves, no matter what the temperature was. This was a bonus in defrosting my frozen energy drinks.

Ed radioed up to me and said the town of Stoney Point was just a km up the road. This was a point of interest because it was a visible achievement on my route map. I remembered seeing Stoney Point on the map before I started this journey. It was a good feeling knowing that slowly but surely, I was moving along. As I pulled into this little town of a few houses and a couple of buildings, there were cars pulled over to wave at me as I passed. I saw about 10 cars and heard about 10 honks. The support and word was continuing to spread. One man was waiting at the end of his driveway to see me. Another man stopped his car on the other side of the street and got out. A third vehicle door opened and all of a sudden I had the full support of three local residents showing me the paper. I said that I recognized that guy in the picture they were showing me, as I smiled at them. It was a Help Me Bury Cancer story that gave them a heads up that I was approaching Stoney Point. They all donated generously and told me to, 'Go get 'em!'

Another lady parked down the street a couple hundred feet to wait for me. As I started walking towards her, she was taking my picture as she waited. During the next short amount of time, I had people running from their houses to donate and wish me well. I had people wishing me luck, telling me they were behind me and even asking how my mom was doing. Here I was, hundreds of kms from my community, with complete strangers wishing me well, calling me by name and telling me they're all behind me. I can't explain the feeling of pride I had. I felt grateful to live in this beautiful and safe province and to be supported by my fellow Ontarian's as I made my way past their homes.

As I continued walking my legs suddenly felt looser. I felt strong and ready to put in some serious kms. I changed my ipod to some heavier, more motivational music, unzipped my coat and base layers and gave it everything I had for the next few hours. Ed and Joey radioed up to me and told me I should be stopping for lunch and changing my socks to a dry pair. I agreed that I needed to refuel and make sure my foot bandages were holding up. As I started to slow to a stop Ed told me I was 24 kms into the day. My goal was 20 kms before lunch so I was happy about that.

When I got into the support vehicle, Ed and Joey told me that I was flying out there, kicking some ass. I smiled as I sat down on the couch to have a drink. Without hesitation, Joey was on one knee undoing my boots, to change my socks and redress my feet. My support team was completely taking over. Their support was allowing me to fully concentrate on the task at hand while they took care of everything else. When calls from the media came in, they set up interviews. They were navigating maps, preparing my food rations, giving me advice and support, and driving five kms an hour behind me the whole time.

At home, my wife Erin was taking care of our boys and doing whatever else was needed, so I didn't have to think of it. My mom was contacting media all along the route, trying to find a place in Ottawa to 'bury' the cancer letters, and looking into possible sponsorship possibilities. She was taking care of everything she could handle. My sister (the web master) was making any necessary changes to the website, making updates to my route maps and handling the facebook and twitter pages. My in-laws were cooking my food at home. We had a schedule, so that every few days they would drive it out to wherever I was. It was a complete team effort to get me through my first day and a half and it would need to continue to take me across the province.

I finished a big lunch, put fresh footwear on and was ready to go again 45 minutes later. My legs stiffened up again. It was a challenge to get down the steps of the support vehicle. Ed hooked me up to the sled and I was on my way again.

I was focusing on what was around me, the beautiful country scenery and houses that I was passing. It gave me a break from the mental focus that I had before lunch. I found I always dropped one arm back to the harness attachments and locked it in place while I swung the other arm for as much momentum as possible.

Ahead, I could see a woman standing on the opposite side of the road. When all was clear, she ran across the street and started running towards me. I turned my music off, removed my sunglasses and smiled as she approached me. The next few minutes would turn out to be the most touching moments of the day. Without saying a word, she gave me the biggest hug of the day rubbing my back while she held on. As she pulled away she had tears in her eyes and said she had been touched by cancer and handed me a note. I opened it and saw she also included a cash donation. She said God bless, turned and walked away. After she left I read, 'some people leave footprints in life, you are leaving cancer tracks of love. Congratulations! Continued success in your journey of love.' I looked up at her walking away, and remember thinking that we both know the feeling of being touched by cancer. I will remember her words always.

As I started on way my again, Ed radioed and said that he was in contact with Chatham Police and they were preparing to meet me at their jurisdiction border. I continued to walk down some long country roads feeling good. Again, at the corner of the next road there were people offering donations from both sides of the street. I had a great conversation with them about why I was doing this. They had heard about Help Me Bury Cancer but hadn't yet read my story. I told them that I was pulling this "CANCER" across the province to gain financial support for the Canadian Cancer Society, and build as much cancer awareness as I could. I told them I was pulling this sled for my mom and any other Canadian battling this horrible disease and that together I believed we could make a difference. The group of people I was speaking to were becoming emotional and said I was doing such a great thing. They gave me a very generous donation.

My new short term goal was to reach Chatham Police. Up ahead, I saw a car coming towards us. I saw the cruiser lights come on and make a sound. It was a really cool, welcoming gesture, from the supportive Chatham Police department. He stopped beside me and I shook his hand and thanked him for coming. It put me back when he looked at me and said it was an honour. Here I was, walking down an unfamiliar road in the middle of winter pulling a big sled with a Motorhome support vehicle following my every step and having Chatham Police not only escort me, but tell me that it was their honour! It was a little surreal to say the least.

Ed and Joey once again radioed to me saying that they heard from home again. They said that Help Me Bury Cancer has reached every Halton Region employee through their newsletter. Of course, the Halton Police had a huge part in making sure the word was getting out. Hearing this news gave me yet another boost of energy. My short term goal of getting to downtown Chatham changed for an hour or so. I couldn't help but think of all my family and friends back in Halton rooting for me. The thought of their support back home was incredible.

Sitting in front of me was a challenging hill that I needed to prepare for. At the top of the hill I could see people waiting for me and that really helped me get up the hill without too much of a struggle. When I got to the top of the hill it was great to have their support. It was also great to see way off in the distance, the town of Chatham (my goal for the day).

I started loading up with carbs again, so I could enter Chatham looking strong and in control of this walk. Another police car came to take over for a bit. I thought that it was an innocent change in shift, however, the officer pulled up beside me and said he was going to get his cruiser washed for the papers. I smiled at him and said I could use a wash myself. He laughed and drove away leaving one police cruiser that dropped back behind our support vehicle.

Up ahead there were local photographers on both sides of the street, before I hit town. Out of nowhere, two more freshly washed cruisers pulled up to safely get me through town. As the pictures were being taken, I had three cruisers and my support vehicle surrounding me. A reporter ran up and asked where my next stop was. I replied, 'Chatham Police'. He said he would see me there. As I entered the downtown area the amount of honks I heard was unbelievable. People were coming out of their houses, businesses, hanging out of their cars, cheering me on. A car passed with a group yelling out, "We love you Mike!"

The cruisers sped up and blocked the first intersection. People in the cars that were blocked were getting out of their vehicles, lining up and clapping. My legs were killing me, but with this kind of support, how could I stop and rest? If I didn't have this support, I would have stopped more than an hour ago back on the road. It showed what these people were doing for me. They weren't only welcoming me into their town, they were encouraging my every step as I moved forward. It was such a proud moment for the Help Me Bury Cancer team that we'll never forget.

As we turned the next corner, I could see the Chatham Police Department and officers outside, waiting for our arrival. I also saw another large group that would turn out to be the media. The first person to greet me was the Deputy Chief of Chatham Police. I was so honoured that he took the time to come out and offer his support to Help Me Bury Cancer. I also told him that it was such an honour being escorted by his officers. He said it was their honour to do so. What a nice man to meet.

I worked my way to the group of media on-site. They had microphones out, with their recorders in hand. They started asking me a variety of questions. I remember feeling exhausted from a tough 40 kms, that I had already completed that day. Over the next 10 minutes the reporters asked a lot of great questions. The last one of the day was the question that hit me the hardest. It was a simple one, "Do you think you will make it?" I paused before I answered it. My legs were shaking, my feet were bleeding. I was having a lot of trouble moving my right shoulder and my calf cramps were brutal. I had to come out of my small thought of just finishing the day, and face a very large question that was more than 800 kms away. Did I think I would finish? I then answered, "There's not a doubt in my mind." As I stood there struggling to stand, I looked them all in the eye and told them that I would do whatever it takes, to accomplish what my team and I set out to do. I told them that I believed this challenge would be 80% mental and 20% physical. I told them even if I was breaking my body, my determination was deep enough to carry me though. They all thanked me as I pulled away and the amazing police escort continued down Main street, to make our way through the town.

I radioed back to the support vehicle and asked the guys how many kms I had done, since leaving the Police Department. I was expecting to hear about seven and then heard the words, three kms. The feeling of hearing that was crushing. It may sound funny but even a quarter of a km matters, when you've been pulling a 125 lb sled for the last 10 hours. I closed my eyes and said, "Oh My God." I was hurting. My boots felt like cement. My legs weren't even lifting off the ground anymore.

Joey radioed to me and said my form had changed dramatically over the last hour. I told him I was fine and kept pushing it with every ounce of energy I had. The police cruiser ahead had to drop back and close the gap between us. They couldn't block the intersections for as long as it would take for me to get there. This actually helped me. It was the first time I had to focus on the cruiser in order to stay on my feet. The sun was going down and rush hour traffic was starting. I feel that every car that passed saw that I was hurting. I saw a lot of people that would just watch me while they cried. I knew I wanted to get to 50 kms on the second day and had to push forward. Once again, I asked my support vehicle, "How many have I gone?" Again, the response wasn't what I wanted to hear. I was still over five kms away from achieving my 50 km daily goal.

It was dark and my legs were locking up, a feeling that I've never experienced before. I took a deep breath and told myself not to panic, that I was doing fine. I repeated to myself that I was a machine, and would continue to dominate this pull. I needed to be there for me, if that makes any sense.

I turned my music off and just wanted to focus on the traffic noise. With the loud traffic noise, the red lights of the cruisers lighting up the night, the encouraging words from people screaming to me, I knew nothing would stop me from getting to my goal for the day. Locked in a fog of concentration, I heard Ed's voice come over the radio and yell,

"Fifty!" I was ready to collapse but to this day don't know why my legs didn't stop at that exact moment. I just kept going, I don't remember any pain or any sounds, I just kept moving.

I don't know how much later I went down to one knee, but I knew it was time to stop for the day. My other knee dropped, too, as Ed and Joey ran out to unhook me from the sled. They put their arms under my arms and helped me to the support vehicle, lifting my legs up the steps. They fed me, and gave me recovery drinks as fast as I could take it. I didn't know where we were but was proud to hear another 52 kms were behind us.

I then jumped onto the computer to prepare my daily blog. I knew if I hesitated I wouldn't be able to do it later, by how tired I felt. We found a parking lot to sleep at and to be a drop off/pick-up point. My father-in-law was on-route bringing a bunch of cooked food and clean laundry from home. He would also be picking up Joey to take home, as he needed to get back to work.

My whole body was hurting. I was even having trouble sitting up, but knew I still needed to do an interview before the night was done. I did my best on a phone interview with a local radio station and then fell into bed. I called home to tell everyone I was okay before going to sleep. This was the first night that I had trouble staying asleep. My knees were aching so much that it was keeping me up. I looked over at the clock and knew my police escort would be back to meet us in nine hours. It was hard to think that in nine hours I was going to do this all over again.

Day 3

I awoke to a glorious morning and beautiful sunrise. Had some trouble getting out of bed. I did some physical damage the day before. Our police escort showed up right on time and I still had to dress my feet. I asked Ed to please apologize to them for the delay, but would be out as soon as possible. My problem wasn't dressing my feet. My problem was bending over to allow me to do so. I added some extra energy bars and drinks into my feedbag knowing I was doing whatever it took before I even started for the day.

I opened the door to the support vehicle and put my hand behind my leg to push it out onto the first step. Those three steps felt like a never ending staircase. Ed was setting up my sled and the officer was watching me come down the steps. He was a new officer that hadn't escorted me yet. Watching me come down those steps he must have thought it was a joke, that I was going to continue throughout the day. I was gritting my teeth as I stood and got strapped in. Giving a wave and a nod to the officer and Ed, they knew I was ready. Out onto the road again, the cruiser jumped ahead with lights flashing and our support vehicle tucked behind me.

The sun was shining beautifully as a long country road lay ahead, sometimes just me and the horses that would run over to the fence to see me. My sled made a lot of noise on the road, when I was dragging it behind me. This would attract the attention of every barnyard animal in the area. It was either they were scared or very intrigued, at the sight and noise of my convoy. As I walked and searched for the right music I knew I needed something else, a shot of motivation, or something just to get me focused. I always had motivation for the overall journey, but seemed to want a daily motivational boost, that I could lock my thoughts on for hours at a time. Just then, I got it! Ed radioed up to me and said he had my mom on the phone. She wanted to read something to me. Ed put my mom on speaker and through our donated Motorola radio's, I found what I needed for the day. It was a Facebook posting the night before. It was posted by a woman that was driving home from work the night before and got caught up in traffic behind me. The post said that as she was coming home she was caught up behind police lights and slow moving vehicles. She hoped it wasn't an accident. As she got closer, she could see the Help Me Bury Cancer banner on the back of the support vehicle. Instead of passing, she wanted to stay behind the action for a bit to take it all in. Once she made the pass, she looked over at me struggling and giving it everything I had. She said she immediately broke into tears, thinking of all the people she was close to that had been touched by cancer. She thought how brave I was, showing the world something we sometimes need, 'strength'. She wished me the best of luck and told me that she would never forget me for the rest of her life. As I listened to my mom read this my eyes filled up at what this woman had written. I think they also filled up because I was looking for something to motivate me that morning and out of nowhere, there it was. I told my mom and Ed, that's what I needed and that's what will push me through this day.

While my mom was still on the phone I found out that she would be interviewed by 1290 CJBK in London, Ontario, later that morning. I was looking forward to that as well, not only for the fact the word would continue to spread in the London area, but because it was a live interview and I'd be able to listen to it while I walked. I told her that she would knock the interview out of the park and that's exactly what she did.

I was starting to get in a rhythm, and my legs were loosening up as I moved east. I was coming up on another town ahead. Ed radioed and said the town was called Thamesville. I was always excited to pull into a town or more populated area. Sometimes just for a simple scenery change, but most of the time there were people waiting for me. This was wonderful for spreading awareness and having the opportunity to collect more donations. However, the biggest reason was to communicate with people. It would give me a chance to let my mind rest from intense concentration and allow me to meet some absolutely amazing Canadians. I was only on my third day and already had the opportunity to meet hundreds of great people who called Ontario their home. People in small towns and on the side of the road that I would never have met unless I did this journey. It was a wonderful thing that everyone I came across was supporting me in every way they could. When I pulled into their area, they would take me under their wing and make sure I had everything I needed. As I approached downtown Thamesville, 'Gimme Shelter' by the Rolling Stones played in my ears. I don't know what it is but to this day every time I hear 'Gimme Shelter', it takes me back to that exact place on the road where I have a perfect visual of the town in front of me.

As I entered the town I received wonderful support from all the businesses on the main street. Shop owners came outside to meet me, some only wearing t-shirts in the middle of February. Again I had that surreal feeling, when a Home Hardware employee came jogging across the street saying, "We're all following you Mike," calling me by name and quoting my website. The gentleman said all of Thamesville and Home Hardware are behind you, every step of the way. As he was saying that, other shop owners and people in the town were making their way over to me to have a chat and donate. I have fond memories of the people and the hundred or so steps that it took me to make it through their town.

As I started making my way onto the long county roads again, I could feel my upper back starting to give out. I felt weak. I reached for as much food and drink as possible to combat the feeling. I felt like I was going so slow it could be perceived that I was going backwards. I pulled over and went into the support vehicle to get more food and to talk to Ed about it. I sat down on the couch and didn't feel like getting back up. My thoughts were scrambling. I have enough food and drinks, I have motivation from a Facebook comment, it's only day three, and I was officially suffering. Ed said to take my time and regroup, to remember to fuel yourself. I felt a little confused. I was bonking and I knew it. I knew this walk was not going to be easy and had mentally prepared for moments like this. I immediately went into concentration mode. I needed to recover from this feeling, get out on the road and put some serious kms behind me. Ed said, "Mike, are you ready?" I looked at him and said, "Yes" but remember that I really wasn't.

As Ed was hooking me into my sled I knew I only had about 30 minutes before I would be able to listen to my mom on the radio. I started to take baby steps to get myself going, until my legs started to respond. I could feel my form was a mess and wondered what Ed thought, as he had a front row view of me struggling, with every move I made. Finally, Ed radioed ahead and turned up 1290 CJBK and I was able to concentrate on the interview for a while.

The radio host talked about the 1-2-3 punch that our family had gone through in recent years with the passing of both my grandparents from cancer and the shocking news of the diagnosis of my mom's cancer. They talked about my mom's cancer surgeries and how she knew that her kids were by her bedside, when she came out of surgery. My mom said she remembered us telling her we loved her and us leaning down and kissing her on the forehead. They talked about why I was doing this. I was doing this for my mom and anyone touched by cancer. My obvious goals were raising donations for cancer research and promoting awareness but she also spoke about me wanting to inspire people with my journey, while hoping people would never get complacent about cancer and continue to fight. My mom spoke about how strong I was and that I should be pulling into London later that night. I was so proud at how great she did but I had a bit of a sinking feeling at the same time. My problem was that I didn't feel strong at all and I pretty much knew without asking Ed, that I wouldn't be making it to London that night. My focus needed to switch from London to Melbourne without hesitation.

I put on the most 'pump you up' music, that I had on my ipod. I continued to eat like it was going out of style and most importantly I talked to myself the rest of the day. Or inwardly, yelled at myself the rest of the day. In my head I screamed, 'ONE FOOT IN FRONT OF THE OTHER, ONE FOOT IN FRONT OF THE OTHER, ONE FOOT IN FRONT OF THE OTHER, ONE FOOT IN FRONT OF THE OTHER' for the next six hours. That afternoon, I threw myself all over the road earning every step I took and never accepting the word quit. Mentally I was punishing my body and asking for maximum output every step. I know that I didn't eat or drink enough the day before and it was hurting me. I didn't panic, I knew I would learn from this and not let it happen again.

I radioed back to Ed and said to tell everyone at home I needed more food. I was already on my third lunch and knew I needed more. The pain I felt through my body was immense. I did whatever I could to ignore it. Walking while pulling a 125 lb sled, probably burned up to 500 calories per hour. If I was to walk a minimum of eight hours per day, I would burn a minimum of 4000 calories in total. That is the equivalent to the amount of calories found in 70 slices of bread! In order to keep my energy up, I would need to consume over two lbs of food per day. The amount of carbs was extremely important to supply that needed energy. I was the opposite kind of 'carb counter'. One that wants more, not less.

I continued to have my 'feed bag' on me at all times to allow for quick access to whatever I needed, while remaining on the move. With these calculations, I expected to shed around 20 lbs on this venture. Definitely not by choice, but it would be challenging to consume enough each day. I was only on day three, and I was already over the 140,000 step mark, with some gruelling weight on my back.

Every car that passed on the never ending roads was honking. It's as though they knew I needed it. I had a lot of cars slowing down, to take pictures. I did my best to stand up as straight as I could, to show that I was in control of the day when the pictures were snapped. The last thing I wanted was to announce that I was struggling on day three.

Ahead, I could see a sign. It was Melbourne. I asked Ed for a km count. He said 49, just as I fell to the ground. All I needed was to eat, drink, blog and sleep. Ed packed up my sled for the night and practically carried me into the support vehicle. We drove down the street and found a junk yard. Ed asked if we could pull into the yard for the night to get some sleep. As soon as Ed said that it was Help Me Bury Cancer, they not only agreed, they also offered electricity if we needed it. Another example of the continuous support we were receiving. The night air was cold and the radio said the temperature was dropping for tomorrow morning. I called home to tell everyone other than needing more food, I was fine. I admitted times of struggle, but would never admit the extent. At this point, I wasn't even admitting it to myself.

I lay in the motorhome that night, cold and in pain, from a brutal day. I had trouble falling asleep, but remember knowing I was looking forward to doing it all over again the next day. No matter what I felt like, I hoped that I was making a difference and connecting with people across our province. That, was what was important.

Day 4

In the morning, my eyes were open but I wasn't awake. What I mean is, my eyes were closed throughout the night as often as they could be, however, I wasn't sleeping. I was resting because I knew I needed to recharge my body as best as I could, but I couldn't sleep a wink. A combination of exhaustion, overexertion and throbbing in my knees were all contributing factors. As the winter wind pounded against the support vehicle, my mind was racing, thinking about how my body would respond when I got out of bed. I kept telling myself that I would never submit to defeat and I would continue, no matter what I felt like. My goal was to mentally overpower my physical effort and recovery.

I heard Ed yell, "Are you ready in there, Mikey, are you up?" It was time to go. If we were going to get anywhere close to London, 50 kms away, I needed to get moving. I slowly reached for my bag of bandages to dress my feet. They were getting worse, as the miles added up. I got dressed and realized I had put my pants and shirt on backwards. When I realized what I did, I got angry at myself. I said, "Damn it, concentrate Mike, get in the zone!"

I asked Ed what it was like outside this morning. He said it was cold and windy. I ate a couple of bowls of Vector, some extra milk, fruit, a couple pieces of bread and a Gatorade gel pack. Slipping on my boots was a challenge. My ankles were twice the size as day one. I picked up my walking sticks, to help me out of the support vehicle, and worked my way down the steps.

I told Ed that we forgot to do a morning video, the last 2 mornings! We both just stared at each other for 10 seconds, then had a laugh. It felt so good to laugh. Our minds were both overloaded and we just weren't thinking. Ed said let's do a day 4 video, when you're ready. He also said to tell people how I felt. He said if you're hurting, then say you're hurting. I told him I didn't want this to become a pity session and have people feel sorry for me. I said I feel this walk is about me being strong for people that couldn't be, or who needed inspiration to help them be. Who was I to complain when there are people feeling a lot worse than me, fighting cancer?

My opening words in the video were, 'It was a tough day yesterday, but today is going to be a good day.' I was gaining support through social media at a pretty rapid pace and needed to be an example that they could believe in and follow, for the rest of my journey. Just standing on the side of the road getting strapped in, I could feel the massive head wind pounding against me. Ed leaned over to me with his face red from the cold and said, "Better you than me, Mikey", again making me laugh and loosening me up.

I was pushing through the wind and radioed back to Ed, to tell him to let me know when I put down 25 kms. Until then, I knew I could just look at my feet and pull. Listening to music, trucks passing, cars honking and my own voice, I drove against the wind as best I could, as hard as I could, with as much determination and drive as I had in my body. I heard static on the radio and was waiting to hear Ed say it was 25 kms and I could stop for lunch and a rest. Ed said he was just pulling over to make a coffee, to keep going and he'd catch up. I never said a word, I just kept moving forward. I wouldn't allow myself to try and guess how far I came. If the number I guessed was too low, it was a mental blow, that was hard to recover from. Then, a pick-up truck pulled up beside me. I was thinking it was another donation. I turned my music down and smiled at him, as I slowed to a stop. He rolled down the window and said he read about me in the paper. He said he thought I was a man with a huge heart, to be putting myself through this. I said that I was just doing my part. He told me that he lost his wife to cancer. I remember his face when he said it. He was trying to be strong for me. I said that I was so sorry to hear that. I also said that these are the stories that I wish people didn't have. He asked me to pull into the next driveway on my right. I waved Ed over in the RV. The man in the truck was a farmer, who was directing our support vehicle to his fuel pumps. He said to fill it up. This was huge for us. The cost of gas driving across the province at idle speed wasn't cheap. We thanked him so much for his kindness. He reached into his wallet and pulled out a crisp fifty and gave it to me in my left hand while I shook his right. I said to jump on his computer ten minutes a day and follow my trek. He said he just might do that. As I was pulling away I looked back at him standing alone on his long driveway and felt for him.

I walked another hour before Ed said it was 25 kms and lunch time. My father-in-law, Kim, was pulling over with us. He drove along the route to find us, bring more food and a full laundry service and had been following the support vehicle for the last 20 minutes. I walked as upright and smooth as possible when he saw me, so he would bring home the news that I looked good.

When I was inside eating lunch, Ed was able to provide me updates of what was going on. He said that website hits, were through the roof. He said media was calling and wanted to drive out and take pictures. London was very interested in my whereabouts, as they heard I was on route. This excited me knowing slowly, but surely, I was working my way closer.

Back out on the road I knew I was in for a long afternoon, again. Then, I heard the upcoming weather. I walked all day with the 35 km winds whipping directly at my face. Now Ed was broadcasting the radio where they said one of the biggest snow storms in recorded history, was heading straight for us. I remember thinking two thoughts. First, I needed to get as close to London as possible. I knew the snow removal there would be better than out in the country. I knew I would trek through whatever old man winter could throw at me but I was worried about the support vehicle on the narrow country roads. Second, was just, 'Bring it!', because compared to what I put my body through in four days, some blowing or deep snow wasn't going to intimidate me. I had prepared for snow. My training included pulling large barn beams through thick mud trying to simulate certain sliding characteristics. I had a selection of footwear to choose from, depending on the weather. I had walking sticks, parkas, goggles and snow pants. I was going to be okay.

I came to the top of a very large hill. Most people would think that's a good advantage going downhill to rest my legs. It was the opposite. I started making my way down the hill. The pressure I felt on my knees with the weight of the sled pushing on my back was agonizing. Up ahead, I could see a parking lot beside the highway that crossed over us. I told Ed that I needed to regroup at the bottom of the hill. I said it felt like my knees were going to pop. While I rested in the lot at the bottom of the hill Ed said that the town of Delaware was up ahead and we'd be there in no time. This was encouraging, as I loved to pull into more populated areas. I started walking again, with my eyes locked on the other side of the road about a hundred meters or so ahead.

A man and woman stood waiting for me, as I approached the border of Delaware. When I got to them, they gave me a cheque. They said that she passed me on the road and drove home to pick him up, so they could come and see me. The man worked the night shift and was sleeping, but he said he wouldn't miss me passing through. They both said they wanted to walk with me for a bit. I thought that sounded great. I had been on the country roads by myself for nine hours or so. I welcomed the company.

My upper back was cramping so badly that I had to come to a stop at times to adjust my movement. They both offered to pull my sled for me. My eyes filled up. I was walking down the road with two strangers that just offered to pull 125 lbs of sled, because they saw I was struggling. What amazing people they were. What amazing people I was meeting. They said that their daughter was diagnosed with cancer at a very young age and they did what they could to help with events and such. I knew then that they would have no problem with pulling my cancer sled. They would have been pulling it for their little girl. I'm sure they could have pulled it with their baby finger. It's the stories like this, that hit me the hardest. A parent telling me their child was struggling. As a parent to two beautiful boys, my heart broke for them. They told me that they have been running an annual charity golf tournament for the last 20 years and donated all the money to cancer research. I thought that was incredible and was so glad our paths crossed at that moment. As we were walking we crossed a small bridge and the couple said, "Welcome to Delaware."

Cars were honking, pulling over and providing donations. I even had a small group of kids ask me for my autograph which made me shy, in a heartbeat. I looked over to my right and saw people flooding out of the Legion. They all were clapping and said they were following me. They asked me to please come in so they could buy me a drink. I pulled over to say hello and thank them so much for the support. I said I would love to take a rain check on that drink but my focus was on London. I had another group run up and donate and started to ask me questions about my walk.

After I answered some questions, a shy boy on his own approached me with his head down. He was quiet and soft spoken. He looked up at me not saying a word. He handed me five dollars, turned and ran off the other way. I started moving slowly to get back on the road, so I could continue on my way. I thanked as many people as I could, which included the lovely couple that took the time to walk with me. As I walked out of Delaware I couldn't help but think what an amazing town it was, with kind-hearted people living there.

Ed radioed up to me and said, "It's getting late, Mikey." I said I needed to continue knowing what my ultimate daily goal was. The sun was setting and I was asking myself for more. My body was saying no, but my mind was overruling it. I wanted London, bad. I kept pushing, and giving every ounce of energy I had, which wasn't much. Ed yelled over the radio, "Looks like only a few more kms to London … go get it, Mikey." It's what I needed to hear.

I was approaching the city that my focus had been on the entire day. All of a sudden, it seemed there were a hundred honking cars at once, in the middle of rush hour. London radio stations had been saying I was making my way to London all day and there I was. It was as though they were welcoming me and saying congratulations at the same time. The 'Welcome to London' sign was up ahead where I stopped and got pictures for my blog. This was the first night that we stayed in a hotel instead of the support vehicle. I couldn't wait. I have never needed a shower and a bed in my entire life, like I needed it that night. The hotel staff were very welcoming and asked how it was going. They all warned me about this massive weather system moving in overnight.

Ed carried the bags upstairs while I hobbled to the elevator. I started with a shower before anything. You would think it would be the best shower of my life, but it was painful. My face and hands were slightly frost bitten, and were sore under the water. My feet were bleeding, raw and hurting, however, I knew I needed it.

I was going through emails that night, from people that wrote to the website. My very first email was from the awesome couple that walked with me in Delaware. They said it was great to meet me and wished me the best of luck the rest of the way. They said they were behind me all the way to Ottawa. I read the second email with a tear running down my face. It was from the mom of the shy boy, who approached me in Delaware. She said she and her son sat in their car on the side of the road, watching me. Her boy asked what I was doing. She said, it looks like he is trying to raise money. Her son said he wanted to donate to me. She told me in the email that she wanted to donate more, but she was a single mom and only had a modest amount to give. She said it looked to her like I was walking for someone, like an aunt or a grandparent with cancer. Her son looked at her with big scared eyes and said, "What if it's for his momma?" They agreed to look up my website when they got home. As she wrote me she said they just finished looking up my story.

Mike Duhacek

Again, her son asked "Momma, who is he walking for?" She looked at her son with tears pouring down her face and said, "He's walking for his momma." They both cried together while they read the rest of my website. This hardworking mom and son wished me the best and said even though her son was very shy, he was going to stand up in front of his class in the morning and tell the students all about me. I think the story and the thought of a mom and son sharing that moment hit home.

Day 5

Lying in bed, most of the night I just stared at the ceiling. I just couldn't sleep. I had to give up the idea that it was the small bed in the support vehicle that had caused sleepless nights before. The light started to shine behind the curtains. It took me about 20 minutes to sit up and work my way over to the window. I actually crawled across the carpet that morning. I grabbed both sides of the curtains and opened it like tearing off a band aid. I knew I was going to see snow but to this day I don't remember ever seeing that amount in one snowfall. Cars and trucks completely snowed in and no traffic out on the road. Ed said he was heading down to start clearing off our ride. I had told everyone that I wanted snow on my trek. But a year's amount in one night? This was going to be a day to remember.

When I walked off the elevator in the lobby there were many hockey teams that were in town for a tournament. I started limping past all the players and parents, making my way outside. I was stared at like I had three heads. I was having trouble walking, I had a frost bitten unshaven face with a large pulling harness on. I smiled at as many people as I could and stepped outside. You could see the look on everyone's face. It was like they were saying, 'Who are you and why are you going outside when we're all snowed in?' Ed hooked me into my sled and said good luck. I turned around to say thanks and saw every person in that lobby at the window taking pictures and watching me. I was not recognizable without my sled attached to me. But once I was hooked up, I think people knew exactly why I was going outside.

I pulled away from the hotel trying to locate the street in spite of the fact that no streets had been ploughed yet. It hit me right then, that this snow storm had shut down the city. It was a ghost town. I now not only had a sled full of cancer, I had a sled full of snow as well. The sled felt so heavy that I really thought that my pull ropes were going to snap away from my harness. I was completely exhausted and I was only five kms into my day. My sled literally felt like 300 lbs of dead weight.

Ed said over the radio that he couldn't believe the amount of snow on the roads, as he idled behind me. The snow was coming down and blowing so much that I couldn't see ten feet in front of me. Ed ran up some ski goggles for me to put on. That helped a bit. He also said that a radio station wanted to interview me, a reporter wanted to meet up and the Free Press wanted to take pictures at Western University today. My focus wasn't the interviews or the pictures, it was trying to pull through the snow to get to them.

My feet were turned completely sideways and I was leaning so far forward to be able to move my sled, that I could touch the ground in front of me. Halfway through the day my body wasn't sore, it felt broken. I was having trouble pulling down a street and got frustrated with the amount of snow and how slow I was going. I aggressively lunged forward in frustration and felt my shoulder pop. Add it to the list of non-functioning body parts. I tucked my injured arm tight against my body to rest it. When I pulled into Western University I spent 30 minutes with the London Free Press on a photo shoot and small interview. The interviewer said, "I'm having trouble driving in this, how are you managing to pull 125 lbs behind you, while walking through it?" I remember my answer well. "I don't know." At this point of my journey I had a lot of different interviews and was actually getting quite used to them. But at that moment while I stood there struggling to stand up, I truly didn't know. That was my answer and I was sticking to it. I answered the other ten minutes or so of questions he asked, so he could write his story. But as far as how I was doing it in my condition? I stuck with my original answer.

I got into the motorhome and sat just staring out the window. Ed said, "Do you want lunch? Mike, you ok?" I continued to stare out the window not saying a word. My injuries and not sleeping might have been catching up to me. My frustration with trying to navigate through a snowed in city could have been a contributing factor as well. I was having a moment of feeling sorry for myself. I caught what was happening and immediately talked myself out of it. 'Who are you to complain? Man up, get out there and continue what you started.' I was hooked in and pulling down the road 10 minutes later. I guess my pep talk worked.

I was making my way to my radio interview with Free 98.1, downtown. They were planning on meeting me outside. I was looking forward to that. On route, cars were now out on the road. What a beautiful reception of honks, people hanging out of their car windows yelling, "Go Mike Go." I had people on the side of the road ask me to stop and take pictures with them. Then, out of the store fronts and coffee shops came a big group of what looked like university students. They surrounded me giving me generous donations, hugging me and telling me I was a frickin' superhero. I thanked them all so much, while I thought in my head that was the last thing I felt like.

Another couple of kms I had some more incredible support from the Cancer Society, standing on the corner with a huge banner. This was also the home of 98.1, where all their staff were outside cheering me on. Cars stopped in the middle of the street to get out and cheer me on. It was a big showing. The radio station interviewer said, "Would you like to continue pulling your sled while doing the interview?" I said, "Sure, if you don't mind me being out of breath while we interview." It was a solid interview with a wide array of questions, cars honking in the background and yes, me completely out of breath trying to cut through the snow which was now heavy slush.

My feet were now soaked, not a good situation for my blisters. I never said anything about them to Ed, because I just wanted to keep moving. My focus now, was to head to the London Police station and then end my day at Fanshawe College. This was my most mentally challenging day yet. I was circling a city in a snow storm which resulted in the most physically challenging day on my body. But I wasn't moving towards my goal, which was Ottawa. My hands were raw with blisters from being wet all day while wrapped around my tow ropes.

Ed said to make a left at the next lights and the police station will be on the right, in about five kms. I was directly downtown and my only choice was to walk in the middle of the road, due to the narrow streets and immense amount of snow on the ground. This was the first time I didn't know if the cars were honking in support, or because I was blocking traffic. I was about one km from the police station when I dropped to one knee. I got up as quickly as possible, telling myself over and over, 'One foot in front of the other, one foot in front of the other'. I pulled up to London Police with a wonderful reception. There waiting for me was the Chief and Deputies with a group of other officers. They clapped as I pulled in. What an absolute honour to have these men take the time to come out and greet some guy who was pulling a sled through their city. I spoke to each and every one of them and told them a few stories from my journey. They all were smiling ear to ear and listening to every word I said. They all donated generously and asked me where I was finishing for the day. I said Fanshawe College. They told their officers to make sure I get there safely. I looked at them when I was getting strapped in to my sled again and thought, what great people. I had some pictures taken, the cruiser lights turned on and we were off again.

One Foot in Front of the Other

Five and a half kms to my finish line for the day. The longest five and a half kms of the trip so far. I was following the cruisers down the middle of the road while I had an amazing interview with Andrew Evans from Fanshawe radio. I was trying to control my breathing so I could answer properly, but I was struggling after 10 hours of pulling through a snowstorm. I pulled a little to the left where there was hard packed snow. Not because it was better sliding for my sled, but because I couldn't lift my legs anymore to take a step. My knees were very swollen so I chose to slide my feet along the packed snow, as though I was skating in slow motion. It was bumper to bumper rush hour traffic going the other way. I was receiving the most donations to date. Every person, in every car down the never ending line, gave me something. Some got out of their cars and clapped as I passed, one foot in front of them. It was very obvious that I was suffering and doing whatever it took to slide my feet forward. This long line of strangers took me under their wing and did whatever they could to get me to Fanshawe. They asked me if they could take turns and help me pull the sled. I had a woman stand crying while she watched me, telling me to stop and rest. I just stared down and told my feet to move. Another officer took over leading the way for me clearing everything in front of me. I turned down the final street to Fanshawe. Ed said "A couple more Mike, a couple more and you'll be there." I was earning every inch on that road.

My final boost of motivation again came out of nowhere. To my left, a flood of people came pouring out of a bar with drinks in hand. They said, "GO MIKE! Keep going!" They told me that I was on TV, inside the bar. They came right onto the street and patted me on the back and slid money into my jacket pocket. This was the first time on the trip I didn't respond to the people that were supporting me. I found my focal point and was in a complete zone. I needed something and found it. My eyes were locked on the movement of the cruiser wheel in front of me. My escort vehicle was taking me where I needed to be. I could tell you the wear pattern on that tire. My eyes were fixated on it. I kept following that tire until it stopped. I stopped and while I was still staring at the tire, Ed yelled, "You're here, you're done Mikey." I looked up and we were in the Fanshawe college parking lot.

I thanked the officer so much for leading the way for me. I felt like her tire guided the way, when I needed it. I got some pictures taken before I got in the support vehicle. I spoke to the officer again and learned that cancer had touched her family, as well. She lost someone very close to her and she said it was her honour to be a part of something like this. I gave her a hug to thank her again before she pulled away. I was done my fifth straight day of my trek across Ontario, with 125 lbs on my back. I was proud of myself for pushing it in and around London for 12 hours. We then headed to a truck stop for the night.

Day 6

Lying in bed in the back room of the motorhome, I longed for sleep. Instead, my mind was racing. I was already envisioning my day. I knew I was going to be alone on some of the longest country roads yet. I knew I didn't have a city or town to shoot for. I knew that I would just walk until I dropped, in the middle of a country road, on my way to Waterloo. That was mentally challenging. My mind set would change from aiming for a destination goal, to just walking until the sun went down.

We headed out from the truck stop at about 7 a.m. to drive to the daily starting point at Fanshawe. I ate extra breakfast and packed extra food in my feedbag. I knew I needed to make some ground today on a body that felt beaten. I was going to do whatever I needed to do. Every morning I allowed myself to think a little bit about Halton County. When out on the road throughout the day I would say, 'Get to Halton' often. Halton was my home and I always said that was the halfway point, even though I knew it wasn't. Mentally, it's what I needed to do.

Ed helped me out of the motorhome when we got to the start point for the day. We recorded our day 6 morning video. I said that it was about 100 kms to Waterloo, smiled and said, "Here we come". I knew I needed to shave off as many kms as possible, trying to get as close as we could to Waterloo. The good news this morning was, that my legs were able to move. The bad news was, they were too stiff to start me off and support me with the amount of weight I was pulling. I prepared for this prior to my walk, when I was in training. I knew I needed to bring walking poles with me to assist me when needed. Ed got me the poles and told me to head that way until you can't go anymore. We both laughed and I said, "Are you saying I'm going to be on some long roads today?"

It was cold, but the winds were low. I knew that the wind wouldn't be a factor and it was just me against the road. When starting out I leaned on those poles like they were my lifeline. I never used them to assist me with pulling. I used them in complete sync with my legs, which would split the difference between my injured legs and arms, to allow better movement. Once I got going and in a rhythm, I felt pretty good. I was happy that my poles were taking some pressure off my ailing legs. These were some pretty remote roads on a Saturday. I pulled for hours, without seeing a single person. I enjoyed it, to be truthful. It allowed me to focus on myself and compensate the injured muscles. I walked on the outside of my feet to rest my blisters. The bottom of my feet were covered in them. I didn't notice them a lot in the day, because something else always hurt more. I walked saying one word over and over again, for four hours. I repeated 'Waterloo' in my head over a thousand times, before I would start again. Doing this would stop me from thinking of anything else.

Ed radioed up and said, "Okay, turn right, you're heading towards Thorndale." In front of me were some pretty steep hills, one after another. I stayed in the same rhythm to climb them. At the top of one of the hills, I saw a man walking towards me. It was the first person I saw that day. I stopped and talked for a bit. He asked what I was doing and where I was going. I answered him and he said he couldn't even fathom what I was saying. He didn't think that would be possible. I asked him what he was doing. He said he had a bad heart attack a couple years back and now he walks every day. He started with walking to the end of his driveway. Then he graduated to walking all the way to his neighbour's driveway and back to his. A year later he walked 2 kms and today he was up to 4 kms. I shook his hand, wished him well and said, see, anything is possible, while I winked at him. I'll always remember the sound of his laugh as we continued on our separate ways.

As I continued down the road, a car passed and turned into a parking lot up ahead of me. I could see a man and woman with their two small children, walking over to the side of the road to wait for me.

As I approached, I smiled, removed my sunglasses and ear buds, to say hello. The couple asked how I was doing. Their beautiful kids handed me money. The woman said she heard my mom's radio interview the other day and completely connected with her story. When my mom gave the website address, she immediately went to the computer to check it out. She saw the route maps and my morning video for the day, and calculated where I would be, so they could drive out to see me. The man shook my hand and the woman gave me a card in an envelope. She said she had breast cancer and thought what I was doing, was nothing short of incredible. I looked down at her little kids, who only came up to my waist. I looked back up at her and put my hand on her shoulder. She was too young, she had kids to raise. I told her I had two little ones at home rooting for me. I told her I missed them. I was just outside Thorndale, talking to a family that knew exactly why I was doing what I was doing. I knelt down to say thank you to the kids, shook her husband's hand and hugged her goodbye. She squeezed me tightly and held on while rubbing my back. It was a Mother's hug, that said thank you and be safe out there.

When they drove away I went into the motorhome and opened the envelope. There was a beautiful picture of her and her kids when she didn't have any hair. Her hair was growing back now and it looked great. The letter said, 'Find strength knowing that there are so many people cheering you on! You are doing a great job for all of us! Not only is your mom (and family) proud of you! But this mom is, too! You can do anything you set your mind to! God bless you, Cyndi.' It was a beautiful letter given to me by a beautiful family. Ed was going to call my mom and read the touching note to her as well.

I was now entering Thorndale. What a cute town and what a warm welcome. It was awesome to see people lined up on the road, cheering me on. I stopped on the side of the road to eat lunch. As I was in the motorhome eating, I had people knock on the door just to meet me, which was again surreal. Another person brought fresh food to us and told me to keep eating, to sustain my energy. The people of Thorndale were so good to us when we passed through their town and I'll always be thankful to them.

I continued on my way, down what seemed to be a road that never ended. The day was so clear and I could see for miles and miles. Eight hours into the day and I was still relying on my walking poles. Pure determination and relentless focus helped my body do, what I was asking it to. A brother and sister pulled over to wait for me. They asked me how I was doing and said they were just coming back from a ski day and had to pull over to say hello. They told me that I was an inspiration and it takes a brave soul to do what I was doing. I enjoyed talking to them for 10 minutes and remember saying that they had some mega long roads in these parts. They laughed and said, 'They seem to go on forever, don't they?' I was so happy to hear that they would not only follow my journey, they would spread the word at the same time. It was these little breaks in the day, that helped me so much.

It was dinnertime and Ed asked what I was going to do, and how much longer I could go. I said I was going to eat and then carry on. I knew I wanted more kms behind me, so I could feel that it was a successful day. As the sun was going down, I glanced over at some country homes that were set back from the road. I saw people on their porches with their arms in the air. I raised my arm at them, as well. I was still connecting with people even though I was walking alone.

The roads were so quiet that night. Ed put the headlights on, so I could see my way. I was at the point of completely punishing my body. I reached for a stone that was attached to my harness since the start of the walk. It was a small stone in a pouch that I gave to my mom when she was fighting for her life in the hospital that said, 'COURAGE'. Before I headed out in Windsor, my mom gave it to me to carry. I clenched it in my hand for the remainder of the day. She also gave me a small quote she had cut out from a magazine. It said, 'You don't know strength until strength is the only choice you have.'

Ed drove up ahead of me to take video of me walking. He started recording, and I said that I had one more hill to get up. I ended up doing a few more hills than that, before collapsing. I was happy with the distance I travelled. I knew I had given it my all. I kissed the rock and placed it back in the pouch on my harness. Ed helped me into the motorhome and we drove to the back of a gas station parking lot, to sleep.

I had a phone interview, followed with a talk on the phone with my wife. She said she and the boys were coming to see me tomorrow night, and that a hotel in Waterloo had donated a couple of rooms, to the Help Me Bury Cancer Team. This was a huge shot of motivation. To know my family were on their way, to sleep in a hotel AND have another hot shower, was music to my ears.

Day 7

I don't think I slept a wink last night. My sleeping habits were getting worse. I sat up and stared out the window at a gas station wall most the night, just accepting that I wasn't sleeping. The good news was that I had the opportunity to take care of my feet, during this time. My sister gave me specific instruction on what I needed to do to keep the infection down. A lot of tea tree oil and needles, followed with the exact recommended second skin, foot and gauze pads. I also had the opportunity to wrap my left knee and my right elbow. Putting a hot rub on my shoulder, I took Aleve tablets to help with the swelling and Tylenol for the pain. This was also the first morning that my stomach wasn't feeling well. On-route to the starting point, I was doing my best to get some food in me. I started with plain white bread and water. Even though the first five days I ate more food than I normally would in a month, I was losing a lot of weight. I knew I had to force myself to eat as much food as I could and to be careful not to become dehydrated. However, the movement of the motorhome was making it difficult to hold anything down. When Ed pulled over and said we were at the starting point he jumped out to set up my sled. I stepped out with him to breathe in the fresh air. I was just wearing my pant shells and a base layer on top. The cold air and wind felt amazing. I stood out there for five minutes and drank a litre of ice water before I finished getting dressed.

I finished putting my gear on and got ready for my blog video. Ed asked if I was ready. I said yes, I was going to talk about my favourite Facebook comment so far. It was a comment that said, 'Crush it'. The message told me to own it and it was exactly what I needed to think and do, this entire day. I repeated that to the camera. When I started out I only used my walking poles for the first km, then I put them both in one hand and swung them for momentum. This was a good sign.

It was cold and visually beautiful as I worked my way up 37th line. The sky was clear and the sun was making the ice covered trees shimmer, as far as I could see. I didn't even have my music on yet, I was just taking in a perfect, quiet morning. I was 10 kms into my day when I saw an older gentleman up ahead, waiting on the side of the road. I had no way of knowing what a great guy I was about to meet. He might have been 70 years old, no more than 5.5 feet and 110 lbs, but he was as tough as they come. He rubbed my back when he spoke to me. He said he had been diagnosed with three different types of cancer in his life time and beat every one of them. I admired his attitude. He wasn't feeling sorry for himself. He said that cancer picked the wrong man to mess with. This old boy was the inspiration I needed! He gave me energy, got my wheels moving inside. We shook hands hard, as I winked at him. When I was pulling away, he said, "Go get 'em Mike!" To this day I don't know what he was doing out there on a Sunday morning in the middle of nowhere, but I appreciate that he was.

I drove it hard for the next couple of hours. Inspired by that survivor, I turned up AC/DC on my iPod and got mad at the road. Tired and injured, I was doing my fastest kms since the start of the walk. Two hours later I was suffering from doing that pace, but didn't regret doing it. I did it for him.

A car pulled past me very slowly, while they took pictures of me. They stopped up ahead. I met up with a wonderful woman who just wanted to talk. Tears were in her eyes the whole time we spoke. She looked about my age and she had kids of her own. She knew why I was doing this and thought it was awesome. That night she liked me on Facebook and wrote that she met an amazing guy today, that had so much passion for what he was doing. Her family turned into a big supporter of Help Me Bury Cancer. I was grateful she took the time to stand on the road and talk to me that day.

I turned down another long road that felt like the longest I've ever seen. I put my thumbs in my harness at chest level. I pulled forward on it every time I took a step, so the harness support put pressure down the centre of my back. This was relieving my back spasms and I was happy I had a temporary solution for this problem. When I saw pictures of me that night, I noticed my posture was terrible. I couldn't even hold up my shoulders. If I didn't know my family was waiting in Waterloo for me, I think I would have stopped and called it a day. This was the first time I allowed myself to consider completing a shortened day. I could barely move forward. Suddenly, a man on a bike out for a winter ride pulled beside me and started talking about the weather. We had a really good conversation as I continued to move down the road. I appreciated him and was drinking up whatever he was saying because I could concentrate on something other than what hurt on my body. He rode away and wished me well. That night, he was tweeting about a guy pulling a cancer sled. He was doing his part. He was spreading the word in hope of helping me with my goal.

Now, my only thought in my head was my family. I thought of their faces waiting for me at the hotel. I told myself they needed me to get to them. That thought allowed me to pull reserve energy from places I didn't know I had it. Down another big hill with horrible knee pain, up the other side with that heavy drag behind me. I wasn't going to take no for an answer. I was getting myself to Waterloo. Up ahead I saw a large sign. I radioed back to Ed and asked if that could be a Waterloo sign. He said he wasn't sure. Pulling the sled towards it, I was praying it was. As I got closer, I could see what it said. I made it to Waterloo when the odds were against me. I made it to Waterloo with the help of the older man, a kind woman, and a guy on a bike. But mostly, I made it to Waterloo because my family was waiting.

My sister Nicole, and my brother-in-law Joey, were waiting at the sign. They knew I would do it. Joey was going to take over driving my support vehicle for the week. Ed was going to head home to go back to work. I got unhooked from my sled and started walking towards my sister. I'll never forget her face. This was the first time she had seen me since day 1. Her eyes filled up, as I tried to walk. She hugged me and told me, lovingly, that I looked like crap. My eyes teared up when I was hugging her, it was so good to see her.

Mike Duhacek

Ed had his bag packed and was ready to leave. I gave him a hug in the motorhome. Again, I was emotional. I don't know what I would have done without him driving behind me, supporting me in every way possible. Saying that Ed had my back the last week, was an absolute understatement. He was taking care of his son, who was walking for his own wife.

I was also happy to see Joey ready to take over the driving duties. I knew he would be putting a protective shield around me, every step I took. I said I needed to go to the hotel. My sister smiled and said Erin and the boys were waiting for me. When we were checking into the hotel, Joey called Erin to say we were there. Erin and the boys were just getting out of the pool. Joey loaded my bags onto a large luggage cart and told me to walk all the way down the hall, to find my room. I could hear my boys in the distance but still couldn't see them. I turned the corner and there they were. My wife and my two sons. What a sight for sore eyes.

The boys ran excitedly towards me. They had never gone so long without seeing their Daddy. When Erin came around and saw me, it was such joy and such pain all in one moment. I could see in her eyes how happy she was to see me, and how much it hurt her deeply, at the same time. I was grasping onto the luggage cart in hope of some stability. I was attempting to walk forward, but could only manage a shuffle. I was exhausted, injured and frail. I also had frostbite. I saw shock in her eyes, but she attempted to hide it by her smile. We stood in the hallway hugging. She was supporting my weight as I had not a leg to stand on. I hugged my boys hard, it was so good to see them all. They all helped me into the hotel room where I was looking forward to finding out every detail of what they'd been up to over the last week.

We got caught up and ate, before I did my blog. They all waited on me hand and foot, throughout the evening. That night while everyone slept, I sat and watched them. The view was a shocking comparison from the gas station wall, the night before. Erin woke up and saw me not sleeping. I told her this was the absolute norm and to not worry about it. It was just nice to rest and get refreshed before another long day in the saddle.

Day 8

Washing up before heading out, a little knock came to the washroom door. It was the familiar knock of my youngest son, saying that he had to pee. I said, "Hold on one sec, Bud", as I hid all my bandages. I knew I was heading out in 10 minutes. Joey knocked on our door and said the police escorts were on their way. It was time to hug and kiss the three of them goodbye and thank them for coming.

As I went outside to hook into the sled and meet the police escorts I knew my family would be heading for some breakfast at the hotel restaurant. I didn't allow myself to think any more about it. It was time for another day on the road. The officers pulled out onto the street and blocked traffic. You could immediately hear the honks starting, as I pulled out onto the street. I spoke to my mom the night before. I told her when I calculated the amount of kms I would do in a day before I started my walk, I really didn't factor in all the stops along the way to talk to people who make the great effort to come out and cheer me on. My mom mentioned that it sounded like a cancer journey, a journey that you couldn't control.

The stories I heard were such an important part of this walk, and I was so happy for the support I was receiving. My website hits were on fire each day. My Facebook likes were growing faster than I ever thought they would, and the amount of people that I stopped and talked to, were double what I thought it would be. This would be my daily motivation. Knowing that word was getting out across the province that a cancer sled was being pulled by some guy who wanted to raise funds and awareness.

Mike Duhacek

The temperature warmed up a bit and the snow was turning to rain. Most people might have thought this was a good thing, but it wasn't. I was used to the cold temperatures and even the snow, but the rain was soaking me to the bone. My feet, once again, were my number one concern.

I received awesome support from some University students who donated and provided some encouraging words. It was also wonderful to see the Cancer Society women come out and meet me on the road to ask if I needed anything and to see how I was holding up. Once we got to Weber Street I knew I had my sights set on the City of Cambridge. This was a good opportunity to change my drenched outfit and footwear. When I went into the motorhome, Joey also said the newspapers and radio stations wanted to interview me. He said that he gave our whereabouts to photographers, who were on-route to take pictures. I changed and ate as fast as I could to get back out there, as the photographers showed up and took shots of me heading south down Weber. A few more kms down the street I had a couple of interviews with a newspaper and a radio station. It was an exciting moment knowing I was heading out of Waterloo and into Kitchener. I really felt like I was covering good ground and getting closer to my home base, Halton.

The heels of my feet were giving me pain. Every time one lifted off the ground, I would feel the discomfort. At this point, I just added it to my list of ailments. I decided to continue to alternate footwear every chance I could, to switch up my pressure points. As I worked my way south, I had patrons from another bar come outside to toast me and tell me I was doing a great job. I then took off from an intersection, and felt the most intense pain I had since the beginning of my journey. An old hockey injury in my right knee reared its ugly head. I started limping badly. I quickly tried to focus my thoughts on what kind of pain many people with cancer endure. They don't have a choice, so why would I think that I did?

One Foot in Front of the Other

Joey radioed and said that my mom was driving out to find us, to bring another banner for the motorhome, as one had ripped in the wind. The day before, I knew my sister warned my mom of my condition, so I had a feeling that it wasn't only a banner drop off. I also knew that Erin would have talked to her after seeing me the night before. My mom wanted to know how I was doing in person. She was waiting up the road on the shoulder. As I got closer to her, the look on her face was one of worry. She never said a word, she just walked over to me with her cane and threw her arms around me. I knew she didn't like seeing me in the condition I was in. She whispered to me, "What do you need? Are you ok?" I said I was fine, I was just feeling weak and emotional. She pulled back a bit and asked if I needed to stop. She said we can end it tonight and tell everyone the truth about how many injuries you have. I looked at my Mom with her watery eyes and stated, "If I have to crawl to Ottawa, I will crawl. I will never quit." My mom's eyes filled up a little more and she said, "Okay kid, then get going," as she grinned at me. She also said that she spoke with Erin about my condition. She said that Erin was sick about it and was very specific, that I wasn't going to sleep in the motorhome anymore. She said that if we had to pay for it, so be it. Not having a proper sized bed and a shower was hurting me. I said I thought at the beginning of the walk that I only wanted to sleep in the motorhome, but after having a couple of nights in a hotel, I realized it allowed me to mentally recoup a little bit. My mom said that my team would make sure I had a proper bed to sleep in every night. I gave my mom a kiss on the cheek and was on my way.

Cambridge was in sight. I could see the sign. Limping down the road I was so proud that I had made it there. My Waterloo police escort had been so awesome. I thanked him so much for being there for me all day. A Cambridge officer was there to meet us and take over. The number and steepness of hills I was going down was unbelievable. My knees couldn't take it. I came up to the next hill and radioed back to Joey and asked him to please unhook me from my harness. Once he did so, I turned my sled around and walked it down the hill in front of me. At least I didn't have 125 lbs pushing against my knees from behind. This was slowing traffic behind me but I couldn't care about that right now. My police escort was handling that perfectly.

As I was making my way down the street, I passed a hospital where I had many people clapping and cheering me on. A mom and daughter were waiting up the road to donate generously. The woman said her daughter wanted to wait for me. She also wrote me that night and said what it meant to them to see me pulling my sled and how emotional it was for them. Joey radioed and said his sister Rachelle was going to work on getting us a room for the night. I was glad to hear she had become a part of the team.

I knew I was getting closer to Halton, when a car passed and opened his window to say, "Go Mike, Go". It was a colleague from work who lived in Cambridge. It was great seeing him. Joey jumped back on the radio and said we don't have just any room for the night, Langdon Hall has offered two of their suites to Help Me Bury Cancer. I didn't know what Langdon Hall was, but Joey said, "You will soon enough". I radioed back and said five more kms, then we'll call it a day. I knew I had it in me, as I kept pulling the sled, the best I could. As I finished the five kms, I felt that I was in striking distance to Halton, if I spread it over two days. Joey helped me into the motorhome, fed me and gave me some recovery drinks. I laid back on the chair and felt thankful, knowing I was heading to another hotel for a hot shower and bed. When we pulled up to Langdon Hall my eyes widened. What a beautiful hotel it was. In disbelief, I asked Joey if this was the place that donated two rooms. I struggled to get to my room, thinking just a few more steps.

Langdon Hall brought all of our bags to the room and said the Lexus was available to us, if we wanted to head into town. They also said that we could come to the dining room for dinner. Joey and I both agreed that he would take the Lexus into town to pick us up our Swiss Chalet food, in style. It's what I was craving and what we both wanted. I had my computer set up on the desk, the TV on in the background and a fire going. I was being spoiled and due to the condition I was in, I was accepting it.

Day 9

As spoiled as I felt, I was standing up looking out the window most of the night, instead of sleeping. As Joey packed up the motorhome, Langdon Hall Management wanted to get some pictures with me, outside their front entrance. It was my pleasure to do so. I was so appreciative for all the staff and what they did for me and another member of my amazing team. We were on the road quickly after that, to head to the daily starting point, to meet our police escort.

I felt as though I had been run over by a truck. Yet, at the same time I was happy that I was in familiar territory approaching my home of Halton. I wrote on my blog the night before that I was planning on hitting the Halton border on Thursday morning. I said I wasn't going to hide that this was going to be special. It's where my home, my family and my Halton Regional Police Services family, all were. I said, "Let's light it up Halton, let's put ourselves on the map!"

I was very quiet, this morning. Joey asked if I was okay a few times and I said, "Yes, I'm just getting ready." I was preparing for another gruelling day to land me that much closer to my ultimate goal. It was cool when I passed a couple walking their dog, who had a newspaper in hand. They waved me down and said I had made the front page. They said tell your mom, that her son is a pretty good guy. I grinned and said she'd never believe that!

The sign up ahead said Flamborough. I had a moment of excitement and raised my arms over my head as a lumber truck drove by and repeatedly honked his horn while he held up his arm like he was saying good for you! Joey radioed up to me to say congratulations. It was these little mind boosts that were so important to the mission's success.

Off in the distance I noticed a woman walking towards me. As she got closer I could see that she was crying. I removed my sunglasses and looked her in the eye and asked if she was okay. She gave me a big hug and said she'd been following me since the beginning. She read my story in the Hamilton Spectator newspaper, before I even left for Windsor. She shook, while she sobbed on my shoulder. She managed to say that today was the year anniversary of losing her beautiful son to cancer. I think she was following my journey as a comfort, to try and do her best to deal with her loss. She said she prayed for me every day and knew that I would make my goal. She said to continue doing what I was doing and I'd be fine. I told her that I was so sorry and for her to do her best to take it one day at a time. My heart couldn't have ached for her more.

Another sign up ahead. In about 100 strides, I was going to be at the 'Welcome to the City of Hamilton' sign. I turned around slightly and gave a thumbs up to Joey, not knowing he took a picture. I posted it on my blog that night. Another reason I posted the picture was because of the car waiting at the bottom of the hill, in the background. It was very cool when the door opened and a girl said she was my friend's daughter. I have worked with her dad for the last 14 years, he was a huge supporter of mine. He was on her cell phone, as she passed it to me. John said that I was doing so well, that everyone was cheering for me and looking forward to seeing me soon. I thanked him and said I was looking forward to it. I had the opportunity to talk with his daughter on the side of the road, which was pretty awesome. I remembered meeting her when she was a little girl, who came into work, to see her dad. I thanked her for stopping and I told her to thank her dad for taking the time to chat with me.

Joey called me back into the motorhome for another phone interview with the local paper. Joey was also busy speaking with Hamilton Police as they were wondering about my whereabouts so they could send an escort, as I was now in their jurisdiction. Joey asked me how I was doing. I said, "Do you know that feeling when you have the flu and you just feel that your body is exhausted? Well, times that by a hundred and that's a start." I smirked and stepped out of the motorhome for some more punishment.

Pulling off the shoulder onto the road I saw someone waving frantically at me. I thought she looked familiar. As we got closer to each other, I saw that it was one of my mom's best friends. Cindy drove from Oakville to bring me donuts, muffins and a hug to say that I was almost home. It really hit home how far I'd gone. Nine days ago I was at the bridge to the United States in Windsor. Now I was close enough to home, for Cindy to run out at lunch and bring me some treats.

A Hamilton Police officer showed up and asked me if I wanted him behind or in front of me. Normally I would have said in front, so I could focus on his tire, but I said to drop back as I was already focused on the road ahead. I knew I needed to push it hard and my eyes would be locked on the ground. There were some photographers up ahead who were getting in position to take my picture as I passed by. When I got closer I would yell out to them, "Do you want me to look at you or straight ahead?" They normally responded that they wanted an action shot looking ahead. I even had one photographer ask if I could put on a face like I was struggling. I laughed and said "I am, my body language is screaming at your camera."

Joey radioed and said, "Five more kms and you'll be coming up on Concession 4, that you'll be making a left on. You'll be on 4 for a long time, but when you pop out the other side you'll be on Highway 6 and will be able to see Waterdown." I was repeating 'Go' in my head, every second. When I got to a hundred I would start again. I must have done that a hundred times. It was that repetitive thinking that would distract me, when I needed my best, but felt my worse.

Taking a left on Concession 4, I spoke with a great guy on the side of the road. He said he did maintenance at Princess Margaret Hospital for 40 years, before recently retiring. He asked me if I knew how many people I would be helping by doing this. He said I would be giving people hope and that was more than any amount of money could give. He shook my hand hard and said, "Good on you, son." Very kind.

Joey radioed and asked if I was ready to stop for the day, I was clearly in striking distance to the Halton border tomorrow. My sister called and said she was going to meet up with us. She said that our donations were over the $20,000 mark, Facebook and Twitter were lit up and the hits on the website weren't slowing down. I wished I could give bear hugs to my whole family. They were all working so hard behind the scenes and deserved so much credit for the mission's success.

Day 10

Today started out pretty cool, my sister took over the wheel on my support vehicle. Joey had to head back to work for a few days. Did I mention what a fabulous family I had? Yes, Nicole, her husband Joey and my step-dad, took personal vacation days to drive like a turtle behind me in the middle of winter across our province to support my every step. The further we went, the busier they were. I heard them talking and exchanging information, as my drivers changed posts. They said it was so busy, day in and day out, with countless responsibilities and duties. They never complained once. Not once! All I heard was, if Mikey can get up day in and day out and drag this sled, I can do whatever else is needed. I was, and remain, so grateful.

It was a special experience to start my tenth day with my sister by my side! This gave me the needed energy without even having to search for it. I pushed it down Concession 4, hard. I don't remember feeling pain, I don't remember blinking. I knew that at the end of this road I was going to pop out on Highway 6, which would lead me to Waterdown.

We met up with our next police escort. The OPP were going to take me across Highway 6 and into Waterdown. My escort officer congratulated me, for how far I'd gone. He was so genuine, a really good guy. He outlined how he was going to lead us out onto Highway 6, saying his main objective was to keep us safe and he was going to do just that. His instructions were, "You tell me when you're ready and I'm going to straddle the two lanes, stop traffic and you're going to step out onto the road, with the support vehicle travelling close behind me." He asked how the reception was when people saw me. I said nothing short of incredible. He said then he'll be ready for a lot of noise. He smiled at me while he sat in his cruiser the opposite way to where we were going. He instructed, "You tell me when you're ready," as he drove off to turn around at the top of the hill on Consession 4. I clapped my hands together, looked back and waved him up. I was ready, pumped and focused. The cruiser turned on his lights, sounded his siren and pulled out onto Highway 6 blocking traffic, while we pulled onto the road. It was awesome, every car that I saw was honking, waving and yelling like they were welcoming me home. Before I left, I was fortunate to be on the radio and in many papers where I received amazing support from my community. Many people knew who I was and what I was doing and it felt wicked. My sister was telling me over the radio that our escort was going to start making his way across the entire road. He said to follow his lead to position ourselves in the turning lane, to make a left at the next corner which was Highway 5. We did just that as a car of teenagers hung out the window, saying, "GO MIKE!"

I saw a lady standing on the side of the road up ahead. It didn't take me long to see that it was my mom with a sign saying, '1 in 3 Canadians will be diagnosed with cancer in their lifetime.' It was the

Mike Duhacek

exact words that were on the hospital wall, that pushed me to do this. I didn't even stop, I just looked over and smiled, blew a kiss and kept pushing it. The cars that were stopping me were people on Facebook that had followed me most of my journey. They were coming out to say, welcome home. Every step I took, they were behind me. My father- in- law was dropping off more food, drinks and laundry. It gave me a chance to eat, to fuel myself and have a drink. While I was doing so, I had two more familiar faces approaching me. It was two co-workers that were supportive of everything I was doing. Esther and Nancy brought me cooked food, drinks, anti-inflammatories for my knee and some encouraging words, that I appreciated so much. They walked with me for a few kms asking about my experiences and telling me that everyone was looking forward to my arrival. I thought it was really cool, and I appreciated it so much.

Nicole said the Halton sign was about three kms up the road. The Waterdown newspaper stopped me for a quick interview and pictures. I said that I was so happy to be here. I continued moving towards the Halton sign off in the distance, driving hard. Put my head back down and got her done. Finally, I was at the Halton border. My home! It felt so good, the best I had felt over my 10 days on the road. My sister did a quick video of me, with the sign in the background. I said that I was at the Halton border and was heading out from Kerns Road and Highway 5, at 8 a.m. tomorrow morning, and I was looking so forward to seeing everyone. The Holiday Inn Oakville, that was beside my workplace on Bronte Road, donated two suites for two days to Help Me Bury Cancer. It was a short day of pulling. I only pulled for half a day because I knew I wanted to start from the Halton border the next morning, making it to Headquarters by 11 a.m. where all my amazing co-workers were going to greet me. This meant we could load up my sled, head to the Holiday Inn, eat, rest and soak my feet for the afternoon. When we arrived at the hotel the staff greeted us to get pictures and find out how we were all doing. The Help Me Bury Cancer team was so appreciative to them for compensating two beautiful suites. I massaged my legs for hours and ate as much as my body could take in, in preparation for day 11. I knew I wasn't sleeping properly and probably wouldn't sleep a wink from the excitement of being 'home.'

Day 11

I found myself with my eyes locked on the clock most of the night WANTING it to be morning. The excitement of being home in Halton and knowing I'd be able to share that with family and great friends. From start to finish, I will remember this day always. I was staring out the window at Bronte Road as the sun started coming up. I was thinking that I would be passing this exact spot, within eight hours or so. I was talking to myself a lot. I was saying to be strong and never look like I was suffering. The people of Halton were obviously my biggest supporters and I never wanted to show weakness. I never want it to be about my struggles and I surely didn't want the people I care about most, worrying about me. I took plenty of pain medication that morning and massaged my legs for two hours, doing whatever I could to loosen them up. I started eating small portions of carbs at 3:00 a.m. to build up my energy for five hours, until my start time of 8 a.m. My sister knocked on the door and asked how I was feeling. I said I was nervous, excited and a bit emotional. She said I was going to have a wonderful day and to remember to enjoy every moment of it. I looked at her while she was saying this and thought, how true. I was preparing to walk through my home turf of Halton, with the residents cheering me on. This was going to be a special day and I was going to do my best.

Driving from the hotel to Kerns Road was quiet. I was getting suited up and envisioning the day. Making a left on Kerns Road was memorable. I took a quick look around and saw a lot of supporters, kids with signs, co-workers in my department who I think of like brothers, Halton cruisers ready to escort me, and family pulling into the lot that

I was starting in. I got out of the motorhome and hugged my five co-workers hard. Every day of my walk one of them would write me to tell me they were all behind me. Every day they told me I could do it. Every day they asked how I was doing and how I was holding up. Like I said, they're my brothers.

I said hello to my escorts and Staff Officer Chris, who was amazing. I was going to be escorted by the unbelievable Halton Regional Police. I can't tell you how much I respect this organization and the people who work for it. They are hardworking, dedicated and caring people. My retired Chief and his wife were there to lend their support. That meant so much. My family got out of their vehicle and gave me huge hugs. I hadn't seen them since Waterloo and was so glad they were going to ride in the support vehicle today. The media was taking lots of pictures and full of questions. Kathy and John, who I work with, were there with all their neighbours and kids, with huge plates of cupcakes to satisfy my carb craving and for Valentine's Day. It was the best start to a day I could imagine.

I was ready to go. I was at the bottom of a small hill on Kerns Rd. As I started pulling my sled past cheering supports, a cruiser drove in front of me with the other one dropping behind the support vehicle. Chris jumped ahead of all of us and blocked all the traffic going east on

One Foot in Front of the Other

Highway 5. As I was making a right onto Highway 5, I smiled and gave Chris a thumbs up as he did the same back to me. I remembered sitting in his office months before the walk, when I first announced what I was going to do. He said he was proud of me and he would be behind me. Here we were and he literally was behind me encouraging my every step. Stopped cars and cars driving the opposite way, started laying on their horns. I had quite a few people pulling over to introduce themselves. I recognized a lot of their names from Facebook. Did I mention how good it was to be home? I passed a construction crew that stopped what they were doing to clap and take video. Up ahead a lady was walking towards me. It was Carla, who I worked with. We had a big hug and she told me I was doing awesome. We walked together towards Walkers Line, talking about my journey. Waiting at the corner was a group of co-workers offering support, who worked out of our 30 Division location. They were cheering loudly and had a massive banner with my picture on it and words saying, 'GO MIKE GO.' It was so great to see them, give them a hug and thank them all for coming out to support me.

Ian, from the Burlington Post newspaper, was also there with a photographer. Ian was one of the first interviews I did, for the 'Inside Halton' newspaper. He also did an interview with my mom and I for the Burlington Post, where we landed on the front page before my walk started. I liked Ian and was happy to see him waiting for me. He interviewed me, while cars were honking in the background. He asked how this whole experience was. I told him that it was better than I could imagine. As I thanked everyone and started heading back onto the road I was having a lot of pictures taken of me. It was awesome to see that on the front page of the Burlington Post the next day, with that exact shot.

I continued along Highway 5, making my way to Bronte Road. Up ahead on my left there was a big group of New Electric trucks and employee's out on the road, waiting for me. This organization is so respectful and classy and they were cheering at the top of their lungs. The President, Roland, came out onto the street and gave me an unbelievable donation for $1,000. He said that New Electric was behind me and I was doing a good job. I was so thankful for their support.

The plan was for the Tactical Rescue Unit to meet me, at the corner of Highway 5 and Bronte Road. They told me before the walk that they wanted to meet up with me and the other escorts and walk with me down Bronte Road to our Headquarters. As a sign of respect, they all had their heavy kit on. When I got to them I gave them a hug and told them that I was so honoured to have them walk with me. We all stood on the corner and talked and had a few laughs. Before we started heading down Bronte Road Chris said that announcements were being made over the Headquarters PA system, telling everyone where I was. He said that they were planning on being outside for 11 a.m. I was looking so forward to it but didn't want to think ahead. I wanted to enjoy the moment.

My entourage was growing. I had four cruisers, tactical trucks and our motorhome surrounding me as I made my way south. My mom and Ed were on the right side of the road, waiting for the motorhome to pick them up. My neighbour was also there, lending his support. The Tactical team was walking behind me on either side, with a heavy battery ram on their shoulders, again showing support of the weight I was carrying, and the mission of Help Me Bury Cancer. As we all approached Headquarters, there were many more supporters. I had people bringing me food and saw my Corporate Services team cheering loudly with their blue and yellow pompoms. I had friends wearing T-shirts with my picture on them and the Cancer Society women were all waiting with another huge banner.

I had a very tall man clapping for me, and I didn't recognize him. He introduced himself as Mike Box and I immediately recognized the name. Mike was an online supporter of mine, who I had never met. He was one of my first likes on the Help Me Bury Cancer site and he made his way to Oakville from Milton with his wife to see me. Mike was fighting for his life. He had a lovely wife and children. And he had cancer. Mike was my age, in his mid-thirties. He brought his beautiful family with him and told me I was an inspiration to him. He and my mom shared their cancer journeys with each other and both gave interviews to CHCH news that day. He said it gave him strength when he logged onto my website every day. He said he felt like I was pulling my sled for him. He walked with me all the way to Headquarters and supported every step that I took to Ottawa. As I write this, I just heard that Mike lost his battle that he fought so hard against. My heart aches for his wife and kids he left behind. I was so very sad to hear the news of his passing. My mom cried when she heard.

Lots of pictures were being taken, as I was about to turn into the Headquarters property. Chris rushed his cruiser ahead again and blocked the traffic at the intersection I was approaching. He was waving me in, while about 100 people joined our convoy to walk with me, showing absolute support, for burying cancer. It's hard to put into words the feeling I had when I saw everyone waiting, at the Regional Centre. People were lined up along the ring road and up on the grass cheering for my arrival. So many people who have their own cancer stories, and wanted to help us. It was an incredible feeling that will be with me for the rest of my life. At that moment I didn't feel tired and couldn't feel any pain at all. This was the half way point I needed. Every person there that day was giving me the needed energy, to continue. I was representing them all. Everyone who wants to eradicate this horrible disease.

I pulled my sled right into the double doors of the building that leads to the cafeteria. Everything was set up for my arrival. I stood at the front of the room with the Halton Police Chief and both Deputies who I like and respect very much. As we were talking, people started flooding in to get a seat at one of the tables. When the tables filled up everyone found a place to stand at the side or back of the cafeteria. The Public Affairs Officer started off by welcoming the Help Me Bury Cancer team and saying supportive words about the mission. Next, he introduced the Chief and called him up to the podium followed by both Deputies, one at a time. The three of them said their own beautiful speeches and told me that the whole Service was 100% behind me. I couldn't have thanked them enough. I stood thinking, what an amazing organization and wonderful place to work. The Public Affairs Officer called me up to say a few words. When I was walking up to the podium I received a standing ovation, that humbles me to this day. I smiled, waved with both hands and gave everyone a thumbs up. I thanked everyone for coming, I told them a few stories of my travels and spoke of how perfect this day was, because of them. After the speeches, I had the opportunity to hug a lot of co-workers and thank them. I was able to get some pictures with everyone and had the chance to be interviewed with the news and local papers who took time out of their day to come and see me, which I was again thankful for.

When I went back outside to get strapped back into my sled, I had energy to burn even though I was hungry. I wasn't used to going that long without food. I ate a few quick sandwiches and a container of strawberries, while CHCH was taking some footage of the sled for their story that night. CHCH said they would be driving down the street to get more video of me in action, when I passed by. I told my escorts I was ready, as they activated their lights. I took a deep breath and started pulling.

One Foot in Front of the Other

Pulled down Bronte Road to cheers and past the Holiday Inn, where their employees were out waving and taking pictures. I felt light as a feather. It was the weirdest feeling after I repeatedly hurt my body the past ten days. I never thought much more about it, I just took advantage of feeling good and nailed down some serious kms. As I passed CHCH on the side of the road, the footage ended up as on TV that night. I was making up some serious kms down Lakeshore Road, where I had driven and walked down a million times before. My mom's dearest friend and her father were on the side of the road clapping hard and taking pictures and video.

I passed by Westdale Road, which meant a lot. My grandparents, who both succumbed to cancer, lived on that street my whole life. I grew up visiting often, and now was passing by it trying to make a difference in the fight against cancer. I knew they would both be watching down on me, beaming from ear to ear, and so proud of both me and Nicole. I kept driving myself hard, where I soon passed the cemetery where they were buried. I put my arm out and my thumb up to mark the moment. My mom and Ed were standing there, yelling, "GO, GO, GO" and clapping for me. A couple of co-workers in my department met up with me to walk for a couple of kms. It was awesome with them seeing me off and telling me that I would make it to my destination and that they would see me soon.

Mike Duhacek

Once I reached downtown Oakville, I started to feel human again. Well, a human with sore muscles, who wasn't sleeping. The day was starting to catch up with me. I kept pushing as I knew if there was anywhere I was going to find strength, it was in Halton. As we turned right onto Cross Ave. I met up with more supporters who were outside of their workplace, waiting to donate. I saw Tim Hortons up ahead and said to everyone that I needed a rest and a couple of donuts. We all pulled in, with a thousand eyes on us. People who knew what we were doing and people who didn't. I ate a couple, well, a few, donuts for the last bit of needed energy. I said goodbye to my wife and sons who were heading home for the evening. I knew that they were going to travel in the support vehicle again the next day so I felt good about that.

I wanted to make it to the Peel border. This was the longest portion of the day, bar none. I was 'done like dinner,' but wasn't going to show that weakness. We kept plugging along until the Peel border was visible in the distance. I was so proud of the kms and strength that I put behind me during the day. My sister said, "Let's pack your sled up and get back to the hotel, to watch you on the News." We drove back to the Holiday Inn and did just that. Nicole also taped a short video in the hotel room so I could have the chance to thank everyone once again. I had a lot of comments sent to me about that video. People said they worried about me because I looked and sounded so exhausted. I said, "Thank you so much, but I'm fine."

Day 12

Lying in bed thinking about what the 12 days on the road would bring, my phone rang at 3:58 a.m. I wondered who it was and what was wrong. I picked up and heard, "Hi Mike, it's Breakfast Television calling." I responded with excitement in my voice, "Well hello, Breakfast Television, how are you?" They said they wanted to do a story on Help Me Bury Cancer and asked if I could meet up with them. I believe my exact words were, "WHERE AND WHEN?" They asked me where I was starting today. I told them that we were meeting the Peel Police at Royal Winsor Drive and Winston Churchill at 8 a.m. They asked, "Can you meet us there at 5 a.m.?" I said, "Yes, we'll see you then." I hung up and said, "Holy Crap!" There was stuff all over my room after two days of staying at the hotel. I had an hour to pack up and get across town to the Peel border. How was I going to do that? At this point I was just staring at the wall. I thought, 'NICOLE!' I had to go next door and get my sister up… immediately. I moved as fast as I could, which was about the speed of a turtle. I banged on her door and called her by the nickname that my mom and I had called her for years, and said, "Todes? Todes, you up?" My sister answered the door and said, "What, are you okay?" I rambled off as fast as I could about Breakfast Television calling and wanting to meet us, but they want to meet us on the other side of town in less than an hour. "CAN WE DO IT?" Wide eyed, Nicole said, "Of course we can do it. Get back to your room and pack up as fast as you can and I'll knock on your door when I'm ready to go." I stared back and said, "K." I'm not kidding when I say by the time I made it back to my room, my sister was knocking on my door saying, "LET'S GO!" I said, "Jeez Todes, help me pack, like quick. Seriously!" We went downstairs and threw the room keys on the desk and hurriedly said, "Thank you so much for everything, but we need to go to an interview." Nicole went running across the parking lot to get the motorhome. The headlights popped on and I swear there was a tire squeal. A full-size motorhome flying across the parking lot to pick me up. I laughed out loud knowing it was my sister driving that big bus. The back door of the motorhome flew open and Nicole said, "GET IN!"

We flew down the road with the Help Me Bury Cancer banner slamming against the side of the motorhome. We didn't have time to take it down from the night before. We wanted to keep the banner on this morning to advertise our cause. We had our fingers crossed that it wasn't going to tear off on the Highway. I was eating as fast as I could. I was suiting up as fast as possible. Getting ready so quickly that morning meant I had no time to bandage and wrap my feet. I was going to have to go without. I was a little nervous about that, but I couldn't find any time. When we got to the intersection, where we were going to meet the Breakfast Television crew, we saw their truck pull into a carwash. Nicole pointed, "There they are, over there." As we drove over and into the parking lot to meet them, we heard a huge bang. I said, "What was that?" Nicole said she didn't know and not to worry about it.

I had an awesome interview with Breakfast Television and they shot some video. They wanted me to stretch near the sled, set it up for the day, things like that. I did my best to look like I could even bend my legs. I felt like saying, 'Are you kidding me, Breakfast Television guy?' I decided to grin and bear it. Then I got the big rundown of how the morning was going to go. They were going to set up, right out on the corner of the street. He wanted me to pull out of the carwash parking lot and head right towards him just looking straight down the road. He said that he would be filming, then packing up quickly, then driving further down the street to set up and get more footage of me. He let me know that all of this was live TV. I said, "Yeah, no pressure, eh buddy?" as I smiled. He laughed, and said that I'd do fine. Peel Police arrived and said they were ready when we were.

One Foot in Front of the Other

Just as we were going to pull out onto the road I saw that there was a chain from post to post, overhead, that supported a car wash sign. I thought, 'Oh no, the motorhome can't make it under that!' Five seconds later the camera man yelled, "Action!" In my mind all I was thinking was, 'Oh no, I'm pulling out of here on live TV and my support vehicle, with my sister driving it, is going to smash into that chain and rip it out with millions of people watching.' I started pulling my sled down the street with my fingers crossed, looking straight ahead, like my interviewer Jeff told me to do. The corner of the intersection was lit up with camera equipment and we were in fact, rolling. With that, boom, smash, clang. I closed my eyes knowing exactly what happened. My support vehicle was trailing me closely with the car wash sign draped over the motorhome roof. I thought, 'Oh man, I hope that's not on TV' as I smiled to myself. It was too late to turn back, the live footage of me walking past the camera was feeding back to Breakfast Television. All of this action was good for me, I had no real time to recover from my high pace the day before but I felt good. Really good. I ate about five carb packs and drank a Gatorade quickly, before Breakfast Television was flying past to set up ahead of us again. I could see way off in the distance that the camera crew was setting up everything as fast as they could. More cars started hitting the roads for their daily commute and were noticing what was happening. Lines of cars either stopping or slowing down, with their windows open, welcoming me to Mississauga and wishing me the best, for the rest of my trip. The Mississauga News was set up on the side of the road taking multiple pictures as we passed by. I went down a small hill and back up the other side as I passed by the cameras again. Nicole was talking to my mom, on the phone. My mom was saying that she was watching the footage and it was looking great. All I could think was, what incredible coverage this was.

As rush hour started, the roads were loud. I believe it showed how many people watch Breakfast Television in the morning. The reason it was a different kind of loud than what I'd already heard, was due to the pure volume of traffic. The Greater Toronto Area was a different animal. It would be a modest estimation, if I said over 75% of people and vehicles were acknowledging us out on the road. The donations were coming in fairly quickly, which I was so happy about.

Nicole radioed up to tell me that our website hits were multiplying every step I took. She told me I was doing so well and to keep going. A van load of people jumped out on the side of the road. They unzipped their jackets and had on the same black daffodil shirts. It was the local Cancer Society coming out to congratulate us. We stopped and talked, and I said it was so cool of them to take the time to come out to see us. They asked if they could get some pictures. It was another overwhelming morning of community kindness for Help Me Bury Cancer. It was time for Peel Police to hand me over to Toronto Police. I made excellent time through Mississauga and was looking forward to being in Toronto.

It was time for my family to meet up with us again. My father-in-law brought Erin and our boys to us. They were going to travel with us through Toronto, which was awesome. I started out with one Toronto escort while I was travelling down the narrow portions of Lakeshore Road. Once I got into the busy, wide open sections approaching Windermere Ave, I had more escorts join our convoy. I had four cruisers on the busiest sections. Two cruisers at a time used their sirens and blocked every driveway in front of me. Another led the way for me, with the fourth one dropping back behind the support vehicle.

Toronto Police had a shield around me, to keep me safe, while keeping traffic at bay.

A sport utility vehicle pulled in-between me and the cruiser in front of me, to pull into a parking lot. One of the officers got out of his cruiser, to ask what he was doing. The gentleman said he had something to give me. I stopped on the road while he ran up to me. He said that I had a ton of support and I was doing an amazing thing. He handed me a brand new Toronto Maple Leafs hockey jersey. The owner of Glory Days Memorabilia wanted me to have it. An avid Leafs fan, I grinned from ear to ear and said, "ARE YOU SERIOUS?" I thanked him for taking the time to deliver the jersey to me. The back of the jersey had #67 on it, with "Glory Days" across the name bar. I started pulling away with my arms out to each side and the jersey draped over my back. It was the perfect gift as I have bled blue and white my entire life.

It was a busy Friday evening. As I was getting close to the street I was supposed to go up next, an officer asked why I wasn't going to go up Yonge Street. I said I would love to, but knew how busy it would be. The officer smiled and said if I wanted to be noticed, then go up Yonge Street. I smiled back and said, "Let's do it!" I radioed to Nicole and Erin and asked if they could post a quick message on Facebook regarding a route change, and said we're heading straight up Yonge Street. They were excited, but at the same time Nicole noted the size of the vehicle she was driving. I asked if she would be okay with it. My sister radioed back and said, "Of course, let's do it!"

As we continued down Lakeshore Road, we came to a complete stop due to traffic volume. It was a chance to talk to a lot of people, who put their windows down or got out of their car. It was also an opportunity for Joey's sister, Rachelle, to come running up with her arms full of sub sandwiches. It was amazing to have her on the Help Me Bury Cancer team. She was on the phone daily with hotels, asking if they'd consider donating a room to Help Me Bury Cancer. I don't remember a time that she called my driver and said she couldn't get anything. If one hotel turned her down, she found another.

My team thought it was good for me to rest, but the opposite was true. My legs were killing me from standing so long, without moving forward. Finally, Yonge Street was in sight. The officer who was going to lead me up the most popular street in Canada, came to chat with me. His name was JC, and he was one of the nicest guys I've met. He lost his mom to cancer, and said he would be honoured, to escort me up Yonge Street. By this time of the day I felt dead in the water. My legs were shaking under me. We started up Yonge and went through the tunnel, to the sounds of horns echoing. When we popped out the other side, there was a group who stopped to clap for us. Our escort JC was flashing lights and sounding the siren, completely in control of the whole situation.

I looked back to see how my sister was maneuvering the beast of a vehicle through the thin and intimidating downtown streets, but she took it in stride. With Nicole driving, and Erin navigating, it was a true team effort. As we were waiting at the intersection to turn left on College Road, I recognized the man who was walking across the street in front of me. We looked at each other at exactly the same time and said, "HEY!" It was the college student who interviewed me at the 'Pink in the Rink' hockey game in Oakville, put on by the Cancer Society. I had been honoured to drop the puck at that game before I started the walk. He pulled out his camera, as fast as he could, and started snapping pictures. What an absolute coincidence that we met up that evening, in the busiest city in Canada.

The Toronto Police Headquarters was in sight. It was a perfect place to stop for the night. I thanked my escort, JC so much for everything he did for us, and said it was a pleasure meeting him. We took pictures outside the station, before we went inside for a tour. I was so proud of my team in the motorhome. I looked over and saw Nicole had parallel parked, in-between two cars on the side of the road. We made it through the busiest part of our journey. It was a good chance to eat, drink and rest after a long day. We packed my sled away in the motorhome and went looking for our hotel for the night. This was the moment that I completely crashed. I couldn't think, I couldn't speak, I couldn't stand and I was having trouble keeping my eyes open. I fell asleep on the bed in the back of the motorhome. This left Nicole, Erin and my boys to navigate and get us to our hotel for the night. I wrote on my blog that night that I was sitting in Toronto ready to explode out of the city tomorrow, and added, 'OTTAWA, here I come!' I said I was going to 'crush it' but wasn't sure I felt like I was, at that moment.

Day 13

My knee was hurting me. Behind my knee was swollen, the size of my knee cap. It was extremely difficult to bend it, or even move it forward. At this point into the journey, I had to accept that I was going to rely on one leg, far more than the other. Erin, and even my young boys were concerned about my condition, but supported me no matter what. My sister told me that we were having problems with the motorhome and she was going to call Ed and Joey before they went to work, to see what could be done. My entire team were always very careful about what they told me. They said my only concern was to concentrate on getting myself to Ottawa and not the things that popped up along the way. Just like every police escort, my family also had a protective shield around me. Within 45 minutes both Ed AND Joey arrived at the Holiday Inn in Toronto to repair the motorhome, so we could keep to the schedule. My sister told me not to worry and to just concentrate on getting my feet taped up. To this day, I don't even know what was wrong with our support vehicle and just know that like everything else, it was taken care of by my unbelievable team. I gave Erin and our boys a big hug, as Ed was going to drive them home now that he was there. I told them that I would see them in no time and I would talk to them that night.

Nicole and I jumped in the repaired motorhome and drove to the daily starting point where I had finished the night before. It was a frigid, windy morning. It was about -15 Celsius and Nicole said it looked like the wind would be in my face for the day. Driving to the starting point, Nicole was on the phone with Toronto Police telling them we'd be there in 10 minutes. When I got out of the motorhome to start my day, there was a woman and her daughter waiting for me. They said they saw me the day before on the front page of the Burlington Post newspaper and drove all the way out to me to lend their support. They gave me a wonderful donation and a Tim Horton's card. So thoughtful and sweet of them. We talked for a bit and got some pictures, before my police escort showed up. My escort and I also talked and introduced ourselves. We went over the route map and had a few laughs. Like all my previous escorts, he was a great person who cared about my journey and doing what he could to help. As we pulled away, it was very quiet on the roads this early Sunday morning, even though I was in the middle of the city. My officer told me that the roads ahead were going to be a steady climb for the next few hours. I said, "Oh yeah, you're full of great news this morning, aren't you?" and we both laughed. I radioed to Nicole and said I was going to do whatever it took today, put my head down, and focus. This morning my plan was to get mad at my sled. I needed to get in the zone. I put my sunglasses on. I knew I wasn't going to have the happiest look while I climbed uphill all morning with the freezing wind blowing in my face. I yelled at myself, 'Battle, Battle, Battle' while I got into a rhythm. I had two simple choices. Give up, get into the motorhome and head home, or climb this hill and fight like hell every inch of the way. I climbed a steady incline for over 15 kms before taking my first rest and refueling with as much food as my body could take. My escorts were now changing, with another Toronto officer relieving his partner of his duties. As I was meeting my new escort, and thanking my other one for everything, I talked about the rough morning with the hills. They both laughed at me and said my route was taking me right up the old Kingston hill. I smiled at them as that meant nothing to me. I said, "Is it a big hill or something?" They laughed while they both said, "You'll see." I can picture the exact moment that I turned the corner and saw this hill. It very well could have been the biggest hill I'd ever seen. I thought that it could be a challenge to walk up it, let alone with 125 lbs on my back, a banged up body and a leg that wasn't working so well. I radioed back to my sister and said, "Holy Shit!" She replied, "Holy Shit is right!"

I slowed down to a crawl so I could sneak in a few gel packs and energy bars. My eyes never blinked, I was locked in and staring at the base of the climb. I wouldn't allow myself to look up anymore. I wasn't going to let this intimidate me. My job was to put one foot in front of the other and beat this hill, whether I was exhausted and hurt or not. I started climbing and could immediately feel the strain on my calves and my shoulders, from the weight of the sled pulling on my harness. It was uncomfortable in every way but I was going to succeed, no matter what. I was suffering half way up and every part of my body was telling me to stop. I screamed at myself, 'You have more, you have more, you have more' as I kept climbing. I did whatever I could to ignore the burn and get to the top. It wasn't pretty, but I did it. I pulled over the top onto flat road, panting like a dog, and dragging my leg behind me. Nicole got on the radio and yelled, "Way to be Mike, you did it!" The snow was starting to come down as I unzipped my jacket, as I was overheating. The cold winds felt good. My whole body was shaking from that climb. I struggled to open my feed bag to get a drink of water. I learned that night that Nicole started taking video of me and doing a short narration of my condition. I saw the struggle in my step when I watched it. As the video was rolling and I was walking in front of the motorhome Nicole recorded, "It's been a day of hills. He's tired and hurting I can tell, of course not complaining, and he's so determined. He's gone 22 kms and not one bit of complaint coming from him. And the next time I think I don't want to do something because I'm too tired, I'm going to picture this. It's incredible." I enjoyed watching the video that night. Not because I enjoyed watching myself struggle, but because it was nice to hear Nicole's perception of how I was doing.

As I continued moving east on Kingston Rd., snow was falling. The traffic was light on this section of road and I was just continuing as far as I could go. I had no specific destination this day. We called it, 'Walk till you drop day.' The support on the roads continued to build, as I got into busier sections. I never got used to hearing people yelling my name from their houses or stopping to donate and call me by name, it caught me off guard. But to have people tell me that I'm giving them hope, or that my journey is helping them with the loss of their child, or even giving them strength to fight their own cancer, was humbling. That was my ultimate goal, to support and spread awareness across our province and even further. To show people that there were people out there fighting for them. To show that I was going to struggle, but also show that I was going to dig as deep as I possibly could to persevere. Hopefully, to be an ear on the side of the road for people to vent to. To be strong for people who aren't feeling strong themselves. It meant the world to me when people understood and supported that.

Toronto Police said that they contacted Durham Police to take over my escort, as we were approaching their jurisdiction. I felt proud knowing that on day 13 of my journey, I had reached the other side of Toronto. At the same time, I knew that my pull from Toronto to Kingston was a long one, that would put me on highway #2 for about five days. My driver could basically point their finger and say, 'Just go that way' day after day. I felt mentally strong and prepared for the challenge. Durham Police was now escorting us. Durham was loud like Peel! I hoped this kind of support was going to continue as I moved east.

Up ahead I saw a familiar face, that made me smile. A friend from Motorola who I worked with the last couple of years, donated the radios that my entire team and I used throughout the walk. The batteries, chargers, clips, holsters, everything. It was an amazing gesture and we appreciated it. We don't know what we would have done without them. Standing on the side of the road, Dave and his wife were ready to support me as I passed by. As they stepped out, I met him and his lovely wife, in the middle of the road for a hug. Dave told me I was doing so well and said they were following me on Facebook, the whole way. It meant so much for them to come out and see me on a Sunday evening.

My sister radioed me and told me that City TV was looking for me. I said, "Cool! Are they coming to find us?" Nicole responded excitedly, "Yes, they will be to us in about 30 minutes and will do a story for tonight's news." This was big. I knew what Breakfast Television did for us. Now we would be given exposure on prime time TV. I was looking forward to it. It was perfect timing for a story. I had car after car pull over to donate. I had cars parked on the side of the road for as far as I could see, at one point. The City TV truck pulled past me and about four cars on the side of the road. They jumped out and started filming. This was unbelievable footage showing anyone watching that it was as easy as pulling your car over, to help me "bury" cancer. I reached the City TV reporter and chatted about my day before we went on to record. He said I would do great and 3-2-1 fired the first question. I thoroughly enjoyed our interview and was grateful to City TV for coming to find me. It was obvious on TV that night that it was cold. My face was the colour of a tomato and the 13 day old scruff on my face, had turned into ice pellets. It was cool to hear the background noise of the people and cars. I couldn't have asked for better coverage. The story was aired just after 6:00 p.m. and the length was generous. After the interview, I felt like I couldn't focus anymore, and was a little disoriented and foggy. The snow was really coming down and blowing in my face by this time. It was a typical Canadian winter scene, while I approached the Durham sign.

Another large hill descent followed by another climb took me to my knees. This was one of the most brutal terrain days I had. I put in a solid day though, that I could be happy about. Mentally this day was a success, I had the mental strength to carry my body over every hill. My driver would change tonight. Joey was making his way to relieve Nicole. That night as I sat at the computer I had multiple ice packs on me, doing my best to sustain the swelling. I wrote on my blog that it would take focus and determination as I moved east. I meant it.

Day 14

I got a little bit of sleep by sitting up last night. I fell asleep with ice packs on and am guessing that my problem areas were so numb, that allowed me to get some rest. I couldn't lie down by this point. My legs could not straighten out when I was on my back and the pain in my knees was awful if I attempted to sleep on my side. Joey knocked on the door and said it was freezing outside. He said the thermometer was reading minus 25 degrees, at this point. This was good knowledge, for how I would dress. I put a base layer on, and for the first time would wear my heavy clothing that consisted of 'Canada Goose' snow pants and my 'Canada Goose' Parka that were kindly donated. I needed to put my harness on under my big parka, instead of over the lighter jacket or hoodie that I normally wore. I also clipped on a pair of gloves to the front of my parka, in case I needed them. We met up with my Durham escort Officer. What a good man. I took some pictures with him and spoke about members in his family who had cancer. He said that he was glad I was the one walking outside today, as it was crisp! I smiled at him and said that I was disappointed to hear he wasn't going to offer to pull my sled today, as all the other escorts before him did. I waited a couple seconds while he stared at me. I winked at him, while we both laughed. I lifted my parka up while Joey clipped the sled into my harness.

 I pulled into Whitby on a crisp and cold, yet beautiful, winter day. It wasn't long before two girls came running after me with Tim Horton's in hand. They handed me a muffin and a hot drink. They said they saw me on the news last night and thought what I was doing was the sweetest thing and wanted to bring me something. I thanked them both very much and said it was so sweet of them to buy me this and bring it to me on such a cold day. They wished me all the best and said they would be following my journey.

Joey came out to get the items and five minutes later we were passing Tim Horton's. A man was walking out of the store with an extra-large coffee and climbed into his car. Just as he was going to close the door, he noticed me pulling past him, 10 feet away. He got out and ran over to me. With coffee spilling on his hands, he gave me the coffee that he had bought for himself. He said, "Please take this to keep warm and God bless you." I said his generosity was appreciated, and he shook my hand. I was so touched by it, I didn't have the heart to tell him I don't drink coffee. However, the good news was, Joey was set for the morning!

Another familiar face was walking right out onto the street as I was making my way along Highway #2. It was my mom's cousin, Fran. I gave her a giant hug and asked her how she was. While we were hugging she said, "More importantly, how are you doing?" We had a talk in the middle of the street and caught up the best we could. Fran said I was doing a fantastic job and that she didn't want to keep me from moving forward, so she walked with me for a bit. We were chatting away as the cars drove by, honking or slowing down to donate. Fran said it was humbling walking with me and she asked what I needed. She said to tell her, as she wouldn't take no for an answer. I smiled and replied, "Anything with carbs in it." She said that was easy and would go to the grocery store and buy me some things and see me in a little bit. We had another hug and she was on her way.

As I continued on my way it was time for a quick escort change, as I approached Oshawa. A blue pick-up truck pulled up beside us and waved us over to the shoulder of the road. A big, strong looking gentleman got out of the truck and walked towards us. He said what I was doing was beyond touching and he wanted to do something for us. We learned that he was a farmer from up the road and he had multiple gas cans in the back of his truck. He said that he would like to give us as much gas as he had, as we continued east. Joey helped him and they emptied multiple cans of gas into the motorhome. He also went into his wallet and gave us whatever he had. We said that we were overwhelmed with his generosity and thanked him profusely. He said he was glad to help and that it was his pleasure. Talk about the kindness of strangers. I started pulling the sled and about 30 minutes later I radioed to Joey and said, "How nice was that, eh?" What caring people there were in every part of the province that we were in. By this time Fran was back, bringing bags of food and drinks. Think of the highest carb things in the grocery store and you could probably find it in those bags she brought. Fran said she would come and find me tomorrow.

Up the road was another nice sight that I worked my way to. Rachelle, her husband and children had a custom made sign. They waved their arms above their heads and cheered with everything they had. They also had a big box of Timbits for the carb burner. I ate the box of them while standing talking to them. My weight was becoming a slight concern with the amount of pounds I was losing. I told them how thoughtful they were to make a sign, bundle up their kids and wait with Tim Horton's treats for me, on such a cold day. I radioed to Joey when we pulled away and said, "That was so sweet of them!"

As we headed east I was pulling with a lot of determination. My convoy would attract a considerable amount of attention from walkers, runners, houses and vehicles. This was about to be my first encounter with an accident, due to people not concentrating driving past, trying to see what was going on. A black car caught my attention as I was approaching a major intersection, as it was driving too fast, being too close to the changing lights while the driver and passenger stared our way. The next thing I heard was the sound of brakes locking up and tires skidding, trying to stop. Then I saw a car coming from the other way. I knew then that they were going to collide. I stopped as the two cars slammed together 10 feet in front of me at a high rate of speed. I remember the wheels of the vehicle lifting off the ground, air bags deployed and the horn sounding. I unhooked my sled as quickly as I could and went to see what I could do for them. Joey and my escort officer were close behind. The women passenger was yelling, "Please help my husband." The driver had obvious injuries that needed immediate attention. While the Officer called for assistance and helped the driver as much as he could, I spoke with the passenger to get her mind off of her husband. I said he was doing just fine and they just had a little fender bender. I told her that help was on the way. I started talking about how cold it was outside today. The woman looked up at me and said that she would pray for me as I continued my journey. I thanked her, smiled and said she better be following me, as she smiled back. Emergency Services was on-site as I backed off to allow them to access the car. As other cruisers showed up to the scene they parked around me and asked if we were okay. I said yes, there was some pieces of the car that were flying around, but we weren't affected. They asked me to get into the motorhome for my safety. As Joey and I were inside, traffic continued to pass. People saw a lot of Emergency vehicles and an accident surrounding our convoy, with no sight of me. A message was posted very quickly on Facebook from a passerby, that my sled was surrounded by Police on an accident scene, with no sign of me.

Mike Duhacek

The Facebook post continued that they hoped I was okay and inquired about me. My sister, Nicole, was monitoring Facebook and saw this post immediately. She called Joey to tell us, asked if everything was okay, and said my mom and Ed were minutes away, to drop off supplies. Nicole said she would call my mom right away to let her know we were okay, before they pulled up to the intersection and saw this. She also said that she would post that we were okay on Facebook, so our faithful followers didn't worry. We were asked to sit in the motorhome for about an hour. This was both good and bad. It allowed me to have a nice break, that I wasn't used to. However, I knew I needed to get as far as possible on this day and the waiting was delaying me. I knew I would be pulling my sled in the dark.

When we received the okay to continue, Oshawa Police surrounded me to escort me out of their jurisdiction. Facebook messages were posted from vehicles passing. They just saw that I was on the move, surrounded by flashing lights. In the evening, when I saw my destination sign, it was a relief. I entered Newcastle and continued one km past the sign to position myself on a side street, for the next morning. I told Joey that I was done for the day and this was a perfect start point for the next morning. Joey said Rachelle was making her way out to bring us a homemade dinner. When we arrived at the hotel Rachelle had secured for us, I was looking so forward to a home cooked meal. When I stumbled into the lobby we received a nice welcome from the staff. A couple approached me and said they supported me through London, many days ago. They said they were on route to visit their daughter and stopped for the night. It was quite the coincidence that we ran into each other again. They asked me if they could take my hands and say a prayer for me. We stood in the hotel lobby at 8:00 p.m. with our heads down, as the woman said some beautiful words. I gave her a hug and thanked her. She told me that she knew that I'd do it. She knew I would find the strength and when I didn't have it, she knew that it would be given to me. I smiled at her. Maybe that's what I needed at that moment.

Day 15

Sitting on the side of my bed at 5:30 a.m. trying to eat, I said out loud to no one that I was going to kick some ass today. I felt like I had energy, this morning. I felt like I had aggression for my sled. In that moment, I truly didn't care how many hills were in front of me. In the town of Newcastle, my plan was simple. Get myself to Cobourg. Nothing more, nothing less. I was in a zone, and I was going to take advantage of that.

Joey pulled out his phone and suggested we go outside and film our morning video and hook me into the sled while we waited for our police escort. As soon as I was hooked into the sled, I felt like I was a horse waiting to explode out of the gates. I felt anger towards the word CANCER on the sled, that I was pulling behind me. It was breaking my body down and it was time for some payback. Our police escort pulled up and said, "It's a cold one this morning." I didn't even feel it. I said, "Let's do this" and started to move out onto the road. We were off, with our sights set on the town of Cobourg. Joey asked how I was feeling. All I said was, "We're getting to Cobourg tonight."

We started out on the east side of Hwy 35/115, along Hwy 2. I was in the town of Newtonville, by 11 a.m. My escort officer was such a good person. He was pacing me perfectly and my eyes were locked on his tire. I could have burned a hole through it. A huge hill was up ahead and I was ready for it. I started pumping up that hill, as cars started pulling over to watch. I was so determined to crush this hill. When I got to the top of it, a silver minivan pulled slowly past me and the driver told me he could not believe the speed with which I got up that hill. I grinned and thanked him. He pulled over up ahead and got out to take pictures. What happened next, was so touching and thoughtful. As I pulled up beside the van, the man opened the sliding door on his van. Sitting inside were three beautiful children. Their dad explained that they had heard about me on the news and they wanted to come and find me. I told them that was sweet, and thanked them for coming. Their dad continued saying that his kids know what it's like to lose someone to cancer, as they lost their Nanna to it. I said that I was so sorry to hear that and that I was doing my best to try and raise funds and awareness for the disease. He said, "That's why we're here, my kids wanted to see your sled and give you their piggy banks." I paused for a few seconds and said, "Your piggy banks?" With that, the three adorable kids got out of the van and gave me every cent they had. I was so deeply touched. I got down on one knee and told the three of them that their money would do something really good and how much they were helping, by giving the money they had saved. Joey got out of the motorhome to take a picture of us for our website, while their dad was doing the same thing from the van door. As I was leaving I told them that they had made my day. And they had. This gave me extra motivation knowing that I was carrying three little kid's savings, that they had entrusted to me. I felt like I had more energy than I did at the start of the day. I continued down Hwy 2 towards Port Hope, hoping the family knew how genuinely touched I was.

My mom's cousin Fran chased us down again with more groceries and supportive words. She greeted me with, "Wow, you're moving today!" I told her I felt strong. I really didn't know where this energy came from, but enjoyed the feeling. After loading up the food into the motorhome, we were off again. I started looking for the next water tower. This was becoming a habit and a mentally stimulating one. It's a real boost when you have a visible target. Every day I was on the road, I would search the landscape for a water tower up ahead. As soon as I could see one, I aimed for it. It was a boost knowing that the water tower would be close to, or even in, the next town ahead. The next one that I spotted, was Port Hope. I radioed back to Joey to ask, to be sure. Joey confirmed it was. My focus and motivation switched from the cruiser's wheel, to that water tower. I went after it, like it was the finish line.

There was a small hill at the intersection ahead. I was going to make a right at the top, and head into Port Hope. Climbing that small hill, exposed another injury in my hip. The feeling left me breathless. Injuries were a constant, which made it natural to immediately start compensating, to allow myself to get up that hill. I turned right at the top and slowed to a stop, to try and shake it out. I put both hands on my sore hip and started to massage it as hard as I could. It always seemed to take longer for my muscles to respond or recover, in the cold temperatures. Car after car began pulling over to donate. Port Hope was supporting our arrival. We didn't move for more than 30 minutes. Cars kept pulling up to donate and wish me well, then moved along one after another. Up ahead, there it was, the water tower I was chasing for most of the day. Under it was a large parking lot, a perfect place to stop for a late lunch.

While I was inside the motorhome removing my harness to stretch my shoulders, I heard Joey talking outside. Joey yelled for me to come out. When I stepped out of the motorhome it was nice to see Deb, a co-worker at Halton Police, and her family. They were on their way home from Ottawa and had tracked me down. I gave her a big hug and said it was so great for them to come and find me. When they told me that they were coming home from Ottawa, I looked at them and asked eagerly, "Is it far?" The silence was deafening. Deb and her husband said, "Um yeah, it's a pretty far drive Mike." I smiled at them both and told them that wasn't the answer I was looking for. Deb said my face looked burned and that I looked like I'd lost some weight. As we stood and talked, I thought of how this was a bright spot in my day, catching up with a familiar face. Deb's beautiful little girl gave me some amazing homemade artwork. It was a picture of me with my sled and at the bottom of the paper it said 'thank you!' It was wonderful to receive and I will always keep it. My legs were so stiff and cramped that I waited for Deb and her family to start pulling away before I attempted to climb back up into the motorhome for lunch.

Joey waited on me hand and foot. He kept piling up food on the table, telling me to EAT. I consumed some large amounts of food, but sometimes it was hard to get it all down. I packed up what I didn't eat into my feed bag and headed out, saying, "Joey, next stop, Cobourg!" I pulled through Port Hope with wonderful support of waving, honks and stepping over snow banks to donate.

As I got to the other side of town, I saw the long country road ahead. I had been so focused on that water tower, that I knew it would be a mental challenge heading out into nowhere, late in the day, when my body was ruined. Out of nowhere, my OPP Northumberland escort pulled up. He was called away earlier to an accident. He circled back, rolled down his window and said, "Need a lead?" I smiled and said, "Would love one, brother." With one quick push on his pedal, he jumped in front of me and activated his lights. My eyes locked on that tire and I said over and over, 'Take me to Cobourg, take me to Cobourg.' The cruiser tires were Wilson. We were moving well, and another cruiser coming from the other way turned up ahead, and waited for us. As I got closer I could see it was a Cobourg cruiser. I grinned ear to ear, thinking I was getting close. OPP and Cobourg were driving side by side, as I entered into town. The media met up with us and did a cool interview. They welcomed me to their town. I said that it was my pleasure and I was happy to be there.

I looked to my right and saw the golden arches. I radioed back to Joey and said, "Oh my God, would you get me a Big Mac and fries and the biggest pop you can buy?" I was depleted and completely craving fats and sugar. When I was done eating, I went over to a motel parking lot to get some pictures taken and thank both my escorts. The motel owner and his family came out and said that they thought what I was doing was awesome. He said that he thought I was awesome, too. I had a nice chat with them in his parking lot and thanked them for their kind words.

We got a fun message on Facebook that night. The school up the street wanted to have all their students come out and meet me, while I passed by in the morning. I was excited and looking forward to that.

Day 16

Opening the curtains this morning, the weather was a mix of snow and freezing rain, which was already making the roads quite slushy. My sled doesn't like slush. As my muscles ached when I looked out the window, I knew it was going to be a long, hard, wet day. My stomach sometimes felt a little nervous, as I knew I was once again going to ask my body to do more than it should. I knew I was going to hurt myself, and that takes focus and mental dedication, to allow myself to do that. My starting point was at the same motel that we ended at, the night before. It was great seeing everyone there again rooting me on before I left and gathering around to listen to my morning video. I said that the weather was cooperating with the snow and freezing rain creating a lot of road slush, but I knew that it was a bit of a concern. I also said that my focus was to get to the town of Brighton with my beard, as I rubbed my itching 16 day old growth. Although it may have just looked like a two or three day growth to some!

I was looking forward to getting out on the road, to make my first stop at Cobourg District Collegiate West. A teacher at the school, by the name of Liz Gibson, organized the visit with me and all the students. As I made my way there, escorted by two of Cobourg's finest, an older lady stepped out onto the road and threw her arm around me, while I kept moving. She walked beside me with her arm around my neck telling me she thought I was pretty darn special. I smiled at her, put my arm around her and said, "Aw, thanks, ya think?" She said she thought my effort and commitment were admirable but neither she, nor any family members had ever been touched by cancer. I stared at her, and for a moment, was speechless. I said that I've met thousands of people over the past 15 days and she was the very first person I heard that from. In that moment, it put things into perspective. The majority of our population was struggling with this disease in some way and I hoped I was making an impact. She wished me well and walked to the side of the road.

I saw the school up ahead. My escorts made some noise, as we swung around the bend to the front of the school, where Liz Gibson was waiting. All the kids started to pour out of the doors to come out and see me. I can't tell you how awesome it was to see the entire school dedicating their time to support me. A younger generation standing outside, braving the cold to listen to me say a few words. It was my absolute pleasure to be there. As I spoke about why I was doing what I was and the reasons that made me do it, you could hear a pin drop. Every one of the students were listening intently and showed us such respect. Before we headed out, I spent some time getting some pictures with different groups of students and teachers. The Cobourg Police department was waiting up ahead. They directed traffic, keeping all vehicles away from me and the students. I thanked everyone for coming out as I was leaving and told them to never stop fighting and to always believe in what it is they want to do. I told them if they wanted something, then go get it. I had some students comment on my website that night and tell me they got a lot out of seeing me. One wanted to become an oncologist and wanted to focus on a cure. It was completely amazing reading that. If I inspired one person on my entire walk, I would have been proud of that. But to have our future generation say that they'll focus their attention on beating cancer, that solidified the reason for the entire walk for me right then and there.

We pulled away and made our way up the road to the town line, where an OPP cruiser was waiting for me. I was again pulling into the country and the long, lonely roads. The snow was beating against my face. There were cars in ditches and the ploughs were out in full force. The only word I could use to describe my next police escort, Steve from Northumberland, is awesome. He asked me how far I was pulling the sled today. I said I wanted to try and get to Brighton. He said, "That's quite a ways up the road, but if you want to get there, then let's go get there." I liked him right off the bat. He added, "Well, get behind me and let's go."

As we made our way up the road, we passed many cars in ditches and others were sliding everywhere. I could feel the road slickness under my feet. It was difficult to dig my feet in, to gain the leverage to pull. My escort's lights were flashing and he was cheating the yellow line, allowing me the whole road to pull on. He also was activating his sirens as we passed every house. Steve said there weren't a lot of people out this way, but the people that were there, would hear us coming.

I was already soaked to the bone. I could feel my wet, beat up, blistered feet sliding around in my boots. I knew this wasn't the best situation to be in, but what other choice did I have? My backup footwear wasn't waterproof, so it wasn't an option. My thoughts were just to push it another 15 kms until lunch. I would take a break, change my socks and put my boots on the heat in the motorhome for 30 minutes. As we drove past houses with the sirens sounding, people came to the window to wave, out on their porches to yell, or the end of their driveway to donate.

Up ahead I could see a small group waiting on the side of the road. When I got closer, I guessed that it was a father and son on their driveway. I stopped when I got to them. They said that they were following every single step I took, on Facebook and my website. We shook hands and I introduced myself. The son was being shy, but the dad spoke up and said his son wanted to give me his piggy bank, with all his savings. I was overwhelmed, and thanked them so much for caring and supporting the Canadian Cancer Society. I told them that their money would most certainly make a difference in someone's life. They also asked for my autograph, I never got used to that. A humbling feeling, to say the least. I am just a regular, down to earth guy. Having people ask for my signature still surprised me. It was my turn to feel shy. I said, "Of course, if you want it, I'll give it." The amount of change in that piggy bank was unbelievable. As I walked away I could feel the weight in my feed bag. Joey could see the straps pulling on my shoulders and radioed up to me. He said to stop and dump all that change into the motorhome, which of course I did, to lighten the load.

I got Steve's attention ahead of me and said I needed to stop for lunch and a sock change. Joey pulled the motorhome over and Steve positioned his car to protect us from oncoming traffic. As I climbed into the motorhome, Joey jumped back and took my boots off for me, tore my soaked hat off and told me to get back to my bunk and completely change every item I had on. My brother-in-law was taking care of me, like a mother. He was making my lunch and putting my boots on the heat, as I changed my outfit. We asked Steve if we could make him lunch as well, but he thanked us and said he had a sandwich. I rubbed my legs for 30 minutes straight. When I stopped walking and sat down my legs would severely cramp and spasm. When I tried to get up they wouldn't move, until I punched my thighs to loosen them up a bit. I knew I had a long afternoon ahead of me, but I also knew I had a wicked escort to lead the way.

We were quickly approaching the town of Colborne. I was looking forward to it, as I was hoping to speak with some people in town. I also knew that once I was on the other side of that town, Brighton was in striking distance. Steve sounded his sirens as we made the turn into the town of Colborne. Groups of people came out of gas stations and corner stores. Staff from the Colborne town building were waving from the windows. An older man was waiting at the end of his driveway waving a twenty dollar bill over his head so I would know to stop.

My standout moment while passing through Colborne, was meeting a nice woman named Rosemary. She said she learned of my efforts while watching Breakfast Television. Across the street was the local spa. Women came out onto the front deck of the business to say hello, with curlers in their hair and freshly painted nails in the air. It was such a friendly town, that I have fond memories of. As we made our way out of Colborne it was time to dig deep.

I was exhausted, soaked, sore and just ready to be at my final destination for the day. I was having moments of completely tuning out. I would find myself in a trance while I moved forward. Then I snapped out of it and wondered how I got there. This kept happening over and over. I needed Steve's support like I never needed an escort's support before. It was like he knew it. I'm sure he could read my body language and dropped back a bit. I nodded to him as he looked in his rear view mirror, trying to say that is what I need and thank you for being here. I just kept repeating to myself, 'Stay with the cruiser Mike, stay with the cruiser.' As the wheel was turning slowly you could hear the crunch of the snow under it. As the snow slid off the tire with each rotation, I was so zoned in that I could count the tread pattern. I don't think my body posture or my face expression changed for hours. I was completely locked in and my body and mind were working together to make sure I achieved my daily goal, even if my body was screaming not to.

I wanted to briefly explain to anyone following my venture how I got across long stretches of road with nothing around. I wrote in my blog that night, 'A Wheel on the Cruiser... The right one is my favourite.' When you're all alone walking through rural countryside for hundreds of kms, you need to find something to focus on. My eyes lock on the movement of the wheel. It doesn't matter what the road conditions are, or if it's blowing snow, cold rain, high winds, or freezing temperatures, all I care about is that wheel. The right one. I focus and lock my eyes on it. I become determined to catch it. I haven't caught it yet, but tomorrow I'll be ready to try again. If that wheel keeps on rolling, so do I. Some days I have followed it for over ten hours, staying completely focused on it. Those cruiser wheels are taking me across the province, keeping me safe, and pacing me when I need it. If you want something badly enough, find your focal point, and go get it! The police from across our province were a huge contributing factor to the mission's success.

My goal at the start of the day was Brighton and Joey said we were coming up to it quickly. I followed Steve's wheel all day long and I was ready to look at something else. We crossed into the town and pulled over. It was late and not a lot of people were out on the street. As we stood on the side of the road, I got some pictures with Steve and patted his back, giving him credit for getting me there. He was very modest and said it was all me. I was so grateful and shook his hand hard before he left. As I stepped into the motorhome, a very nice mom and her two young children came over to meet me, which was sweet. I explained what Help me Bury Cancer was about and noticed the mother's eyes were filled up, staring at me while I spoke. I bent down and spoke with her kids and thanked them for coming over to see me. I told them that I would be back here in about twelve hours to do it again. My feet burned, my body ached. I went to the back of the motorhome to my bunk to get my socks and boots off as fast as I could. I began the slow process of tending to each blister.

Day 17

When we pulled up to the spot where we had stopped the night before, we had a visitor waiting for us. The wonderful mother from the night before had purchased groceries for us and was waiting at the starting point. I gave her a big hug when I got out of the motorhome and said she was so kind to do this. Her eyes were filled up as we spoke. It was obvious that this mom was touched by a son doing something like this for his mom. She wanted to make sure I had enough healthy food for the day. We stood there and spoke about her husband being stationed in Ottawa with our Canadian Military. I told her that he sounded like a good man and wished I had the opportunity to thank him and shake his hand. I gave her another hug and said it was so sweet of her to do this. She wished me very safe days ahead and stood back to watch me head out for the day.

Joey had the phone ready for a quick morning video. I thanked everyone who was supporting me and asked people to keep the supportive messages coming. The messages I read at night were helping me so much and I appreciated every single one of them. I also said my goal was to get to Belleville by tonight. Joey hooked me into my sled as I selected some music on my I-pod and mentally prepared to once again force my body to move when it was saying it didn't want to.

It was go time. As I was pulling through the little town, Sean Kelly of mix 97 Radio came running out to interview me. It was very early in the morning and he said he was so glad he caught me, before I headed out of town. He conducted an awesome interview and was a really great guy who seemed like he genuinely cared about the success of the walk.

I pulled away, now focusing my attention to finding a water tower or a sign that said Trenton.

We had a photography and journalism student contact us and say that she was doing a story on me and would like to follow us for the day. She said she would come out and find us on the road, park ahead and wait for us. I always thought it was very kind when someone was going to go out of their way to meet me. It was a cold morning out. I could always judge the temperature by my face and feet before I really got moving. Once I was moving, I never felt a bit of cold on any of my body. I also got word from Joey that my mother and father-in-law were on-route to bring more food to us, which I appreciated. I was eating like a horse, but still losing a pound a day on average. My muscles on the back of my legs were screaming at me. I radioed back to Joey and said I was hurting today. He said I was doing great. Up ahead on the road was a girl who stepped out and started to take pictures. She had multiple cameras on her and it was a good bet that it was the photography student who was meeting up with us. She stood in front of me while I approached her and took picture after picture as she slowly walked backwards. I finally stuck out my hand and introduced myself. She said, "Can we interview as we walk?" I said, "Of course, no problem at all as long as you don't mind me breathing heavily." We had a good interview, as she continued to snap pictures. I was almost to Trenton. She said she would drive ahead and meet up with me later.

When I entered Trenton, I received a lot of supportive honks and claps. My police escort said that it was all over the radio that a man was dragging CANCER right down the 401. We had a bit of a laugh at that, but I was glad the radio stations were picking up the story. A lady stepped out onto the road to greet me. Her name was Evelyn Wilson. Evelyn asked what I was doing, as she had never heard about my trek. She walked along with me as I explained to her that cancer had touched my family and I was sick of sitting around and watching people suffer. I told her that I was dedicating my walk to my mom. I felt an instant connection with her for some reason. Evelyn opened up to me, and told me that she lost her precious 15 year old daughter, Katie, to this awful disease. I stopped dead in my tracks and turned to her. I could see the hurt in her eyes. I felt sick for her. I told her that I wished so much that she didn't have that news to share. She said she wished that she had heard about my trek earlier, so she could have organized something at the high school. The high school that Katie went to. I gave Evelyn a hug and thanked her for sharing with me. She wished me the best of luck and told me that she would be following me all the way to Ottawa. And she certainly did. Evelyn turned into a loyal supporter on Facebook for the rest of my journey. When people called me a courageous person for doing this walk, I knew they got it wrong. The definition of a courageous person is Evelyn Wilson.

Day 18

This morning when I stepped outside I felt the bitter cold whip through me. It was -25 degrees. I stood at the bottom of the steps to the motorhome shaking and staring at nothing, waiting for someone to tell me what to do. I started to think about putting another layer on. With temperatures this low it was a challenge to not dress in clothes too heavy. I had to accept that I'd just be cold for the first hour if I chose lighter gear. As I start to pull my sled, I heat up to the point of unzipping my base layers, and removing my gloves, to avoid chills from sweating. Regarding my feet, I have to consider which socks, which shoes or boots to wear, whether the roads are wet or snow covered, what the forecast will be late in the day, and whether I need to protect my blisters, depending if they're open or not. I can't dress for the temperature only, as I need to factor in strenuous exercise as well. Yes, it can be a bit of a challenge.

I was on the corner getting ready for an interview with Steven Jessel of EMC news before heading out of Belleville. Steven was really good, and we chatted about the last 18 days and some of the experiences I had, making it about a 15 minute interview. By the end of it, Steven said he was freezing and was having a hard time thinking that my day was just beginning. I smiled and shook his hand, thanking and telling him that I would warm up shortly. My police escort pulled up. Todd from Belleville Police would lead me out of town. He was awesome. We chatted and got some pictures as I got hooked up to the sled. As I started pulling and stepping out onto the road, Todd was out there in a flash, blocking traffic. I straightened up and settled in, while Todd positioned his cruiser in front of me. It took about 5 minutes to get used to what speed I would travel at, but we quickly got in a rhythm and were rolling. There was a lot of traffic on the roads with the morning commute, and lots of support with horns and screams of, "Go Mike." Construction crews stopped what they were doing and stood in a line clapping as we passed. We were already approaching the escort hand off point to Tyendinaga Police. When we stopped, Todd and I got some pictures with each other as we held up traffic a bit, but no one seemed to mind. He said he wished he could take me further, but Tony from Tyendinaga would take care of me. Tony was a big, strong guy with a huge heart. He offered a firm handshake and told me he was proud of what I was doing. Tony drove beside me a lot of the time, talking about anything that came to mind. It was a different experience but I liked it. I was concentrating on his voice and not the pain I was feeling in my ankle. We had lots of cars pulling up to Tony's driver window and donating. We were approaching another transfer point where the OPP would take over for the day. Joey radioed to me and said I needed to eat. We pulled over and stood on the side of the road. Tony said that my brother-in-law was doing an amazing thing. Joey said, "Not me, it's Mike that's doing everything." Tony said, "No, you are supporting your family, taking the time off work to be here for Mike and doing whatever it takes and that's why you're amazing." I loved hearing that and appreciated him saying that so much. It was so true and a highlight in the day for me to have others recognize that.

A pickup truck pulled up to donate and the OPP cruiser was waiting to go. Joey told me I was halfway through the day already. I said great, but was trying my best to get my head around pulling this sled for another 5 hours or so. We had a lot of open road ahead of us and I knew it would be a struggle every step of the way. The wind was strong and pounding against my face and chest. My body was hurting and my mind was foggy and tired. Joey came over the radio and told me to go straight. A mom and her teenage daughter came to the end of their driveway to donate and tell me they've been following Help me Bury Cancer the whole time. They said they didn't know how I was doing it. Frankly, in that moment, I didn't either. I told my police escort that I was hurting. Bill from the OPP was a gruff guy. He looked me in the eye and said, "You're the one that chose to do this." I looked back at him and broke

Mike Duhacek

into a hard laugh. His honesty was exactly what I needed. I continued along the road laughing, looked over and saw Bill crack a smile before he pulled his cruiser ahead and threw the lights on. I knew once again I was in good hands. I also knew I needed something else. Music was one of my lifelines. There were days when I wanted music that would motivate me, and days I just wanted old favorites. I'll admit there were times that I just needed a distraction and went straight for a guilty pleasure like 'Built This City,' by Starship. There were many times when I repeated that song, and can remember playing it as I climbed or descended a hill. I even pulled my earbuds out when my favorite songs were playing if I associated them with some moment of pain I had previously experienced. For example, I stopped the Rolling Stones and replaced it with Eminem, because I needed to adapt to whatever the moment called for. Even songs I normally loved, I might not want to hear again a few seconds later. I knew it was the headspace I was in, and just accepted it.

Joey radioed and reported that I'd be able to see Napanee shortly. I immediately thought, Napanee, Avril Lavigne? I yelled back to Joey, "Avril Lavigne?" Joey laughed and said, "Yes Mike, Avril Lavigne." I made a connection, I didn't recognize where I was but it made the town I was approaching a little more familiar. Meghan, from the Napanee Guide, was waiting for us to do the last interview of the day. Meghan had some solid questions and I was thankful my tired mind had the ability to answer them. We were going to have Swiss Chalet for dinner. We made it. Another day behind us and I was so excited.

Day 19

This morning started in Napanee, with my sights set on Kingston. I stuffed myself with a few Tim Hortons breakfast sandwiches, to try and maximize my fuel intake right off the bat. I was losing a lot of weight that I could not only feel, but now could see. As I was getting ready for my morning video, I stood there feeling sick from forcing down more than I was hungry for. My body was beaten. I had strains, pulls, swelling and blisters, and felt completely exhausted. I was cold and missing home.

My brother-in-law, Joey, was setting up to take the daily video, while I stood dazed, looking off into space. Suddenly he said, "And go." Turning my head slowly, I looked at him, and then the camera. What he said, started to register. His hand and arms were moving in a circular motion, basically saying, let's go, the camera is rolling. I said, "Ah, what? Sorry, what?" Without hesitation Joey laughed, stopped the camera, and yelled, "What are you doing?" I started to grin. Again, he repeated, "Are you with me, can you hear me?" in a comical voice. Then it hit me out of nowhere. I became hysterical. Punch-drunk, like I've never experienced. I bent over laughing so hard I was gasping to catch my breath. Joey's words, timing and facial expression put me over the edge. Now the challenge. I had to try and get it together to do my morning video. Take one I got a few words in and lost it. Cut! Take two, I maybe got a word in before losing it again. Cut. Take three. Not even a word in this time. I was bent over, laughing as soon as the record button was pushed. Cut. Take four. I broke into the video the best I could, holding back laughs. With glossy eyes, I explained that I didn't have a good sleep, but I had a good breakfast. Every single day I look for something, anything for motivation, a thought that I could keep my mind focused on for hours at a time. Today I got that, and then some. It was the release of endorphins that I needed, giving me the badly needed rush of positive energy. I posted those blooper videos on my website and facebook page that evening, to show I was okay, and that there's always room for a laugh no matter how you're feeling and no matter how challenging the situation is.

All hooked into my sled and ready to go, my first steps were going to be up a long steep hill, which was becoming a habit in this beautiful part of Ontario. I was hoping this would be the worst of them today as it took so much out of me, each time I encountered them. I climbed that entire hill with a smile. Today my instructions from Joey were to go straight, until I heard from him again. Keeping it simple worked for me. With my exhausted mind, it was just what I needed. My drivers always tried to keep me on the shoulder of the road for safety and flow of traffic, which was appreciated and understandable. However, I liked to drift onto the road as much as I could, as the sliding characteristics of the sled responded better. Every second and every inch mattered. Today the larger stones on the side of the road weren't helping me. So, when I did venture out onto the road a bit, I'd get a reminder in my ear from my awesome driver, quickly adjusting the support vehicle, positioning it so I would be protected from traffic.

As I approached the next driveway, a man with a large beard was standing there smiling. I stopped and put my hand out to shake his. He handed me a donation and introduced himself as Pete. It was great to have the opportunity to meet him and get to know him, while we visited for 10 minutes or so. Pete lived between Napanee and Kingston his whole life. He shared a story with me that gave me another boost. Pete said that someone very close to him was diagnosed with cancer at 17 years old. Then he said that she was now 32 and cancer free. As I started pulling away from him, yelling back how good it was to meet him, another car was pulling up. The man that got out, had three cameras hanging from his neck. It was a reporter, Ian, from the Kingston Whig. Ian and I had a wonderful interview and he took 20-30 pictures. He had been up the road at the Scotties Tournament of Hearts

Curling event in Kingston, when he heard we were making our way towards him. He said he wouldn't miss the opportunity to interview Help Me Bury Cancer, which sounded pretty cool. I liked him, I enjoyed talking to him and thought he posed some great questions. One of his questions was blunt, asking how old I was. I answered 36. He asked if I considered that young or old to do such a physically demanding thing. I said that I thought it was the perfect age to be doing this, that having the combination of physical and mental strength, was an absolute necessity.

The passing traffic was getting noisy. I was approaching Kingston, and they heard through radio and TV promotion, that we were going through their city today. It was a bit humbling that hundreds of cars honked, people ran up to shake my hand, or donate and walk with me for a bit. I had two Kingston Police escorts, Jamie and Jayson, who were amazing. They took us though the busy Kington streets, with our sights set on the Kingston Police Headquarters. I was so out of breath and tired that I wanted the opportunity to stop for a rest. I was looking for a place to pull over, but it seemed like there wasn't anywhere suitable. It was busy with the evening rush hour traffic. I was screaming at my legs to keep moving, to chase down the cruiser. My legs were screaming at

Mike Duhacek

me to stop. I was folding. My legs shook and my right knee kept giving out. Joey radioed and said, "We're almost there Mike, you're doing great." I had tears in my eyes from pain and exhaustion but just wanted to get there. Within the next km we would pull into Headquarters and I could start exhaling. My feet stopped taking normal steps and started shuffling and sliding on the pavement. When we stopped, both Jamie and Jayson asked us to come in. I wanted to and always intended to, but I was done. I had to decline. I needed to get in the support vehicle, badly. But how could I? My legs felt like cement and I couldn't bend them at the knee. After my two escorts shook our hands and gave me a lovely keepsake, they drove away. I could then let my guard down and tell Joey that I couldn't climb those three stairs, and that was the reason why I wasn't already in there. He didn't hesitate for a second. He picked me up and carried me up the stairs. There are no words to explain what I was feeling that day. I don't know what I would have done without him.

Day 20

I didn't sleep well through the night, but I told myself that at least I was resting. I spoke with Erin when I got up, inhaling and absorbing every word from her. Looking at the forecast, I saw it was going to be a rain/snow mix to start the day. I would begin the day at Police Headquarters and would soon find myself pulling through downtown. I went at a slower pace and took it all in, waving to some storekeepers opening their shops for the day. I glanced over at a coffee shop and saw a lady running towards me to wish me well, before leaving Kingston. She said she had been reading my daily blog. That was nice to hear.

I pulled up Tragically Hip Way and made a right so I could head out of town. Soon I was walking past Fort Henry and then the Kingston Canadian Forces Base. I waved at some Canadian Forces members who were yelling, "Good luck, Mike" as I passed. I appreciated that so much.

My goal today, was to get to Gananoque. It was achievable and gave me something to lock on to. I also knew that Joey had a couple more days of driving before my step dad, Ed, took over for the final stretch. As silly as it sounds, I tried to block anything other than the last stretch out. If I allowed myself to think of the final stretch it was a mental error. I had to concentrate on the next step, not the final stretch. I took my earbuds out this morning, as I felt a bit tired of music. I went to my feedbag for a pick me up and grabbed an energy treat that I've been eating a few times a day since the start of the walk. I tore open the package, smelled it as I brought it to my mouth and instantly felt nauseous. I couldn't force my mouth to open, I was so done with it. My father-in-law was driving more food out this afternoon and I was excited about that. I seemed to always be eating and eating a lot. There was very little traffic this morning, it was so quiet I could hear myself breathe. I'd count and see how far I could go, in between each breath. I had a good rhythm going and was enjoying the sight of such gorgeous countryside. Walking along the length of Lake Ontario, seeing the St. Lawrence River, and Howe Island, I was drinking in the sight of majestic trees and rolling hills, reminding me once again how fortunate I was to live in such a beautiful province.

A man was waiting up the road. As I approached him, he stepped towards me. He said, "Let me help you with that." I stopped and introduced myself. I said, "Hi, I'm Mike." He replied, "I know, my name is Chris. I came to help you pull your sled. I'm a postman. I'm strong and I can walk a long way." I put my hand on his shoulder and told him how nice that was, and that I was touched. He said it was nothing, he was angry as he lost his best friend to cancer last week, and wanted to do something. I told him I was so sorry to hear that. I looked at him and said, "Walk with me, but I will continue to pull the sled on my own. It's something I need to continue to do." I told him to feel free to yell at the word, kick it, spit on it, whatever he wanted. Chris grinned and thanked me for what I was doing. I could see that he was hurting as I shook his hand. My father-in-law pulled up to the support vehicle then, to restock the food supply. Chris continued on his way and I took this opportunity to have lunch and catch up on any news I could from home over the last few days. Bags were stocked with high carb and protein-rich foods, and I was grateful for that. I ate like I hadn't eaten in a month. Not stopping to heat it up or even use a fork, I just ate. We talked about Erin and the boys and that they were driving out in a few days to meet us on the route. I was so excited for that, as I missed my family.

I knew I needed to focus and get back out there. Joey got off the phone and said EMC media was driving out to interview me. I said great, I felt good for the time being. I was full, I had great news of my family coming shortly and I had a new stock of food in the RV. I grabbed a milkshake from the fridge door and hobbled down the RV stairs. Joey hooked me into the sled. I thanked him, said goodbye to my father-in-law and started pulling, all while loading up on more carbs.

Lorraine from EMC drove up and pulled in ahead of us. She got her microphone out and was waiting for us. It was an enjoyable interview. Lorraine asked me how many more days until I got to Ottawa. I told her that I was just trying to get to Gananoque, that's where my head was at. She smiled, understood what I was saying, and quickly re-phrased her question. She said, "How long will it take you to get to Gananoque?" I told her that I was hoping to be there by dinner. Lorraine said, "Best of luck, it isn't far. Well, by car" she added with a laugh.

As I was walking down the road, I saw a sign up ahead, and realized it was the Leeds and Thousands Island sign. What a gorgeous part of Ontario. It was my first time there, and the scenery was breathtaking. The next couple of hours went by quickly. Joey said we were approaching the daily goal. Then I spotted it, Gananoque! A mother and two young girls were standing under the sign. The mom welcomed me, and introduced herself and her two daughters. She said I was doing a wonderful thing and that my mom must be proud. I thanked her as we started walking together. She said it was important for her and her girls to walk a bit with me. It saddened me to hear they just moved there after she lost her husband, and the girl's father, to cancer. She said it was hard but they were doing their best. I put my hand on her back as we continued to walk and said how sorry I was to hear that. Looking down at the two precious little girls, as a dad, it broke my heart. I thanked them all for taking the time to come and talk with me. It was a pleasure to meet them, and I admired her bravery.

I spotted the hotel that we would be staying at for the night, as I pulled up the last hill. A man was running towards me with a small child. The dad said his son wanted to meet me. I leaned down to talk to him and said how great it was to meet him. He was a shy and sweet boy, reminding me a bit of my son Jesse. It made me miss my boys even more, but I was so pleased they had introduced themselves.

Mike Duhacek

When we arrived at the hotel Joey unhooked me, helped me inside, brought all of our bags in, packed the sled away for the night and checked us in. I am a true believer in the saying that there is no 'I' in team. Just like there's no 'I' in this walk. My handlers (which is how we jokingly referred to my drivers) were nothing short of incredible. Whether it was my brother-in-law, step-dad or sister, they took care of me in every way. They drove 5 km an hour, keeping me safe, telling me where to turn, giving me never ending encouragement, preparing food, taking calls from the media, calling the police escorts when we entered their jurisdiction, setting up my sled in the morning or even helping me with putting on my shoes and socks when I couldn't. Yes, each one of them was not only my 'handler', but my rock. I truly can't tell you what a huge and very important part they played in this mission.

Day 21

I might have had an hour of sleep last night, at best. The back of my knees were so swollen that I couldn't straighten out my legs. I couldn't sleep on my side either. Stacking a couple pillows under my legs, I laid on my back and took a few over-the-counter pain relievers. I pushed myself to get up every hour or so to walk off the cramping in my thighs and calves. I would sometimes stand by the window if there was any view. Lying down just wasn't the answer at that point. I asked Joey if he wanted to go down for breakfast. Help Me Bury Cancer made the front page of the newspaper, that we saw in the hotel restaurant. We received some nice welcomes and well wishes. My step-dad, Ed, was on his way to take over the driving duties from Joey for the rest of the walk, so it was nice to chill and have breakfast with Joey.

Before getting hooked up to the sled, Parliament member Gord Brown approached us to introduce himself and offer his full support. It was great talking with him, discussing some of the highlights of the walk and some of the reasons why I was doing this.

As I started pulling out, Joey and I were discussing my daily goal. I told him I needed to close the gap from Gananoque to Brockville the best I could, so I could enter Brockville tomorrow. I knew I was going to be on remote roads in the country all day. My plan was simple, walk until I drop. I was extremely determined to give it my best. It was one of those days that I would pull an image that was burned in my mind, whether I want it there or not. It is a memory of walking into my mom and Ed's house to see how she was doing. I found her sitting in a chair, unable to get up. Any time my sister and I ever walked into a room where she was, she jumped up excitedly to come and see us, as she loves us with everything she has. But on this day, after she had returned home from her third surgery, the pain she was experiencing was brutal. She was so pale, so thin, and so very weak. I felt hesitant to touch her she seemed so fragile. I asked what I could do for her, but she just said, "I'm fine, sweetie." But I knew she wasn't, and it hurt me to see her like that. Even though I wanted that image out of my head, I used it on certain days when I needed extra strength. On the days I struggled the most, I put myself back in that spot in front of my mom's chair, and it would give me the power I needed to take another step. I didn't want to do that, but it's an example of the discipline I needed.

A couple hours into pulling, I realized that I'd only seen a few cars. I thought I'd count how many would pass us in the next 30 minutes. At the end of the 30 minutes, there were zero.

Up ahead, I could see a woman come out of the tree line at the end of her driveway. A couple of white dogs came running up to me excited and a bit hesitant from the sound and look of the sled, I assume. The woman was very talkative and seemed like such a nice person. She said she saw me on the road yesterday, but had an appointment to get to so couldn't stop. She told me she then went on our website and saw that the route map said we were going right past her house, so she thought she'd wait for that. I smiled and said, "Here we are". I started petting her dogs as she told me that she grows her hair for six years, then donates it in the name of cancer. That was so cool to hear, and immediately put a smile on my face. I asked her if she had done it more than once. She said, "Yes, this will be my seventh time." I blurted out, "Wow. It's safe to say you've made a real difference in people's lives." Thanking her for the talk, I started on my way, knowing that I had to keep moving forward.

Joey radioed up and said Ed was almost there. I was excited to see Ed, but at the same time I knew I'd miss having Joey with me, too. We pulled over so Joey could pack up, and Ed could bring his stuff in. Saying thank you to Joey just didn't seem like enough.

Ed was anxious to get caught up on any updates, like how I was feeling, did I have interviews lined up, how many roadside donations and how far I had pulled today. I was at the 30 km mark and Ed and I thought I had enough in the tank for a few more kms today. Snow started to fall and blow across the road as I continued on the route to Brockville. I removed my jacket and started pushing it as hard as I could go. I knew what was 18 kms away.

Ed radioed a couple hours later and said, "Are you ok? Are you going to keep going?" The sun was setting but now my mind was locked on Brockville. I kept plugging and plugging, until I saw the sign I had been waiting for. As I pulled up to it, I radioed back to Ed and said, "Stick a fork in me. I'm done." Ed yelled through the radio, "BROCKVILLE!." This was a huge mental boost for me. A 48 km day and I made it to the place that I was trying to close the gap to. I pulled into the Brockville Golf Club parking lot to rest, eat and secure that location for my starting point for day 22. Jenn Ferguson from 104.9 JRfm had requested a live radio interview tonight. Ed and I packed up and headed to the hotel for the interview. While at the hotel, I also spoke to my family and to the Principal of Brockville Collegiate Institute about stopping there in the morning to speak to the school. I was happy to do so and looked forward to it. I completed the 20 minute interview and then jumped onto my blog to report to everyone, that I had made it to Brockville.

Day 22

I woke up this morning smiling. I was excited to get ready and head out on the road, with my first stop being Brockville Collegiate Institute. Ed was up early getting a coffee and planning the route for the day. It was good to have him back by my side for the next few days. We left the hotel and headed for the Brockville Golf Club. I sat on the bed at the back of the RV preparing my feet, wrapping my knee and ankle and re-packing my feedbag knowing it was going to be a long day. We pulled into the Golf Club to get the sled out and do a morning video. It was a struggle to get down the support vehicle steps but felt nice when the fresh air hit my face. I felt a bit sick this morning, like every morning, from the lack of sleep, the overexertion and mass amounts of foods I was eating. Not to mention the motion sickness of the RV. As funny as this sounds, my most comfortable place to be was outside, strapped in and pulling the sled. I was ready to go, started walking up the road and Ed pulled in tight behind me.

Brockville was fun, with lots of friendly waves, cheers and honking. Ed pushed the radio button and held it down so I could hear what was playing. My interview from last night was on. It was surreal to say the least, pulling my sled, listening to the interview and hearing strangers on the street saying, "Go, Mike, you can do it" and "Welcome to Brockville." We were so fortunate to be receiving a lot of donations as we worked our way to the school. When we pulled up to Brockville Collegiate, the students, the principal and teachers were pouring out the doors. Everyone formed a large semi-circle in front of me. The principal I had spoken with the night before introduced himself and talked to me briefly about the timing of the visit, questions from the students and his few minutes introduction to Help Me Bury Cancer. He was friendly and welcoming. I started off by thanking everyone for not only taking the time to meet me, but for coming outside and doing it in such cold weather. I said how excited I was to be at their wonderful school and have the opportunity to meet them all. I spoke for about 10 minutes on why I was doing this, and the importance of committing to something and seeing it through. How courage is having fear and confronting it.

The students had a lot of amazing questions. A young boy in the front of the crowd stepped forward and held out his hand. I opened mine as he dropped a small amount of change into it. His name was Nathan. He told me he just lost his grandpa to cancer and wanted to donate his money to me. I was proud of the bravery of that little guy to do that. I told him I was sorry to hear of his loss. The principal said they had something to present to me. Two young girls came to the front and said how awesome Help Me Bury Cancer was and presented me their bright red Rams school t-shirt. I thanked them appreciatively and took some pictures with them. As I was getting strapped back into the sled, I told the school what a wonderful experience it had been for me to be there. That 30 minute stop was inspirational for me and a perfect way to start the day.

Mike Duhacek

Nathan and I both experienced the loss of our grandpas to cancer. I'll take a minute here, to take you back to 1985. I was at my grandparent's house on their front lawn. My grandpa looked at me. "Want to race to that basketball post over there?" I grinned as we lined up toe-to-toe, and listened for my grandma to say, "Go!"

We ran as fast as we could, and he started to slow down when we got close to the finish line, laughing. He was a competitive guy, being born the middle in a family of six athletic boys. He jokingly yelled out, "Is that all you've got kid?" As we were a competitive family his victory lap was expected, and I laughed as hard as he did. He always had a great sense of humour, and thought nothing of teasing his 8 year old grandson. I loved it, because he always wanted me to give my all. Thinking back to memories like that, I wonder if I did run as fast as I could.

Over the past 22 days of pulling this sled, I have felt like I have reached my limit countless times. When I feel like I have, I have to overcome a limit barrier and make myself break free of it, to show myself what I can do, not my pre-conceived notion of what I can do. When I'm having a hard time taking another step, I hear my grandpa's voice asking, "Is that all you got kid?" My answer is no. And I know he'd be proud of that response. But, I know he'd be proud either way.

Our police escorts led us though the rest of Brockville and out into the country. We stopped and talked as we got to their jurisdiction line. Ryan, Serge and Justin were such nice guys who provided a great escort. They told me there were some very long rural roads ahead of me. I knew there was, as I had reviewed the route map before the walk and expected this section to be a challenge. I was now in a position where I just needed to put my head down for a couple of days and get it done, knowing that Ottawa was at the end of this two-day road. I went five hours hard before my first break. Erin and the boys were on their way to Ottawa to meet me and I was going to get to them in a hurry.

I was dialed in. It was about seven hours since my stop at the school, when some cars pulled up, full of the kids I had met in the morning. They had asked their parents to come to find us. They donated and said good luck. I was touched by them going out of their way to do that.

One Foot in Front of the Other

I pulled for another couple of hours, ending the day in the middle of nowhere. At least, it felt that way to me. My right ankle was giving out, and I remember thinking it just needed to last a couple more days. A car pulled up with a family in it. Parents and their three children came for a chat with me. After the mother saw us on her way home from work, she picked up her family, telling them, you have to see this. We all stood on the road while I told them about how I got there. They were a lovely family and a pleasure to meet. They pulled away and Ed jumped out of the RV, unhooked me and helped me inside. He got me recovery drinks and food, and removed my boots and jacket.

When I was writing my blog that night, I wrote to Nathan, the student from the school, and told him I donated ten steps of the walk today to his grandpa.

Day 23

Stepping outside the RV today was a different experience. We were in the middle of nowhere and you could hear a pin drop. I don't think my eyes blinked, and I gave only short answers to Ed's questions. My body had to listen to me carefully today, because I was going to go get it. Ottawa was within reach.

I did a quick video and told everyone I was focused. Closing my eyes, I just breathed. I was sore, exhausted, and physically and mentally drained, but I had never felt as focused or determined as I did on this morning. I knew that if I walked until I dropped, I could place myself in striking distance to the burial site the next day. I pulled my sled with my beat-up body to get my fastest kms per minute, since the start of the walk. I never turned any music on all day, I spoke to myself over and over again telling myself with every step to go get it. Go get it, go get it, go get it. I repeated it over 43,000 times. I would not allow myself to think. I was in a steel trap of concentration, along the most isolated roads of the walk. When I did come up on the towns of North Grower and Grenville, I had amazing support that I was thankful for, but my eyes were on Ottawa. Where the sign was, how much longer until I got there. Ed said that a major snow storm was on its way that would be so bad that it might not be possible to pull the sled tomorrow. I told him I would pull no matter what. My eyes were locked on the edge of the road waiting for that sign. Suddenly, there it was, what I had been shooting for this entire time. The sign read 30 kms to Ottawa. Ed took my picture as I passed and pointed to the sign.

When I looked at the picture later that evening, it looked like a different guy than the pictures in Windsor. I lost over a pound a day and my body was hunched over, but I made it. By the time I stopped for the night, I positioned myself 25 kms from the burial site at the Canadian Cancer Society in Ottawa. My family was there and they had made it before the snow storm. I was going to get to see them all. Ed helped me into the RV and we headed to the hotel. When we pulled up to it, I saw our truck, then I saw Erin and the boys. I immediately filled up and couldn't get out of the vehicle fast enough. I shuffled towards them with a huge smile as they came running towards me. They hugged my skinny, beat-up body and I hugged them back tightly. We had such a wonderful night together and had lots of time to catch up. My boys went down to the vending machine and got me lots of ice for the back of my knees.

Day 24

I laid in bed resting, but not sleeping, as I had been listening to the snow and ice storm all night. The winds were strong. I thought that this would probably be my most challenging weather day yet. I couldn't quite believe that as of today, I had been on the road for 24 days. I sat on the end of the bed and tended to my feet, and strangely enough, realized I was getting good at it. I kissed Erin and the boys goodbye and told them I'd see them soon. Ed knocked on the door and I knew it was time to get going.

Driving to the starting point was quiet and felt routine. I put on my outer layers, packed my bag with food and slid my harness on. The forecast was nasty and the wind slammed the RV. I pulled my hat on and my hood up, opened the door and stepped out. The door blew shut and slammed against the frame. Ed got me hooked in, said good luck and I was off, heading straight into the wind. Every step was a struggle. I only had about 20 kms to master this day, but I knew within the first few minutes that it was going to take a lot of effort.

As I continued up the road, Ed took a short video of me from the RV, pulling the sled. He said how bad the weather was and how cold it felt this morning just being out a few minutes to hook me in. Up ahead, a lady was fighting the wind and doing her best to open her car door. She stood at the side of the road waiting for me. When I caught up to her she said that she was a friend of Evelyn Wilson, who I had met on day 17. She said that Evelyn had asked her to give me something. It was a $20 bill, and she said that her donation was on behalf of Evelyn's beautiful daughter Katie. I hugged her and said thank you and told her to please thank Evelyn as well. I held onto that $20 bill for the rest of my walk. I thought it was very fitting that Katie's ended up to be my last roadside donation.

I radioed back to Ed and asked him how far it was to the Cancer Society. He said about 10 kms. I was a bit ahead of my prediction from a week or so ago, that said I would arrive the next day. We were going to make that stick, so I would pull for five more kms and leave five kms for tomorrow so I could walk the letters, C-A-N-C-E-R, in and give them the burial they deserved. I pulled over to a gas station at five kms away from the Cancer Society. It felt incredible. I was almost done. I had travelled over 900 kms in 24 days with 125 lbs on my sled, just like I had hoped.

It was mid-afternoon and we headed back to the hotel to actually have a bit of down-time with our family. Albert at Bay Hotel had kindly offered us a couple of suites for two nights, so I could rest before our trip home. When we checked in, they treated us like gold. The staff was wonderful and gave me some personal keepsakes that I'll always keep. The woman behind the desk also gave something to my mom, that she still has.

Mike Duhacek

My family and I all gathered in one room to toast the walk and unwind for a bit. I struggled to get a word out when I raised a glass to my team. I was emotional. They had all sacrificed so much, expended so much energy and dedicated so much time to this. Even if I could get out what I wanted to get out, it wouldn't begin to sound like enough. They all went above and beyond and I love them all.

Burial Day

When I woke up on 'burial day,' I was in a state of disbelief, knowing that it was the day that I would finish what I started, and bury the misery I had dragged behind me for 24 days. The misery of that word that had exhausted and hurt my body, the word that so many of us fear, and that so many people have either beaten or succumbed to. The bright yellow, six letter word, C-A-N-C-E-R, that I had dragged over 900 kms though the roughest of winter conditions, trying to symbolize the struggle in my own small way of how and what it can make someone feel. Weak, tired and alone. One powerful, scary word that connected me with a province, hearing stories from people of things they should never have had to endure. But I also thought of the positive things, including hearing such inspirational messages of hope. I couldn't help but reflect on the hundreds of hours that I had spent on the road and the unfailing support I was offered along the way.

As much as I was happy with the completion of this mission or as much as I had missed home, I had a strange feeling of missing the walk already. I wouldn't miss the blisters or weight loss, but would surely miss the connection that I had made with thousands of wonderful people across our beautiful province. Not waking up and hooking into the sled? Yes, there would be a feeling of relief for that, but I couldn't help but think of those people that can't simply 'unhook' their cancer. So many brave souls that don't have a choice but to get up day in and day out and fight with everything they've got. The true warriors. Other than one woman on day 16, everyone I met was affected in some way by the disease. Whether it was a friend, a family member or themselves, I saw for myself that the sign that I had read saying one in three Canadians will be diagnosed with cancer in their lifetime, that pushed me to do this walk, was accurate. Since my walk, I have learned it is closer to one in two people who will have cancer in their lifetime. Having the pleasure to meet and be supported by so many along my route I say with great hope that we will beat this. Together, we will change that one in two number. We must never give in and never stop fighting. This walk solidified that we are all one team and that every fundraising event, every donation and every single cent counts, in the fight back against this frustrating disease. My Chief and Deputies from the amazing Halton Regional Police, called to congratulate me. Such dedicated men, who offered me such overwhelming and generous support.

Then it was time for me to get onto the road, strap my sled on and walk this word to its grave. My family (other than my mom and brother-in-law) would all travel in the support vehicle behind me, on this morning. It was a short five kms to the Canadian Cancer Society in Ottawa. Usually, my legs didn't even start to loosen up until five kms. But today, that wasn't a concern. The media was there to take pictures, and I enjoyed the supportive words and waves as we approached the final turn. The Cancer Society building was now in sight, on the left-hand side of the road. I spotted the crew and construction equipment that would dig the hole, some supporters and my brother-in-law up on a snow bank, taking pictures. CTV news was also there to do a story on completing my walk. They broadcasted a story of a man starting out in Windsor with his sights set on Ottawa and now would add to that story and air that he had made it to his destination. Pulling up to the driveway I heard lots of cheers, saw lots of smiling faces and the one face that had the biggest smile of all. My mom. We both filled up and gave each other a huge hug. My mom cried and said, "You made it Mikey, you made it."

The hole was now being dug and it was time for us to fill it. I unbolted the letters and walked them over to where my mom was now standing. We threw the first three letters, the C, the A, and the N, into the hole of dirt in front of us together, followed quickly by the last three letters, the C, E, and R. Finally, there it was, deep in the ground where it belonged. People I had met along the route flashed through my mind, as I threw the first shovel of dirt on the letters before the backhoe finished the job off for us. This gesture was for all of them. This was for any cancer patient and their family. But mostly, this was for my mom who inspired me with her own journey and showed me what strength really was. I said a few words to my steadfast supporters and did some interviews.

It felt gratifying and it was now time to celebrate, to reflect and time to spend quality time with my wife and children who were with me in spirit every single step of the way. I wondered how I would start to thank everyone. I decided a start would be to post a message that night. This was what I said, 'First, thank you to my beautiful wife and children. Your unconditional love and support is what made this journey possible. You are everything to me.

To all my faithful followers and supporters, each and every one of you, thank you!

Thank you to the police who offered escorts along the way. You have kept me safe, and kept traffic and safety concerns at the forefront of this walk.

Thank you to the media, who have been generous in their air time to me, and have told my story in newspapers all along my route.

Mike Duhacek

Thank you to Lisa Dale, of the Canadian Cancer Society, for your great enthusiasm and positive attitude.

Thank you to every cancer patient who graciously shared their story with me. Your bravery knows no bounds, despite being dealt a difficult hand, and I applaud you all for that. And to those of you who have lost loved ones, may you all find peace in your heart.

I began this walk wanting to turn my frustration into something positive. Mission accomplished! This walk has raised money for the cancer society, and hopefully showed cancer patients and their families that we all care, and will continue to fight to bring an end to this devastating disease, that takes the lives of 75,000 Canadians each year.

Thank you to my second family, the HRPS.

Thank you to all the companies listed on our sponsor page for the beautiful gifts in kind. Thank you to David J Myers, for his generous cash donation.

Thank you to Rachelle, for becoming part of the team.

Thank you to my in laws, for all you did to ensure I was taken care of with courier trips to our locations to bring supplies and with helping to prepare food for the mission.

And now, to the rest of my family team, to my mom and sister, for working tirelessly on Help Me Bury Cancer for these past months. My sister the web master! Thanks T!

Thank you to Joey, Ed and Nicole for driving my support vehicle day after day at 5 kms an hour!

And thank you to my mom, who has supported everything I've done in life. The one who taught me to just keep putting one foot in front of the other.'

Life Goes On

Waking up the next morning and getting out of bed was, of course, a slow process. I shuffled into the washroom and looked in the mirror. I was scruffy, wind burned and very frail looking. I had a shower and got dressed, as I knew I wanted to go for a walk. But this walk would be a little one. I saw the day before that two blocks away was a Starbucks. I was going to get myself and Erin a morning tea. As I worked my way down to the hotel lobby and out the front doors I started walking towards my destination. After about a block and a half I soon realized that this "little walk" that I was on didn't feel so little. One block felt like 20 kms. It was a weird feeling being on a sidewalk instead of the road. I wasn't strapped into anything and I had no support vehicles surrounding me. For a split second I thought, why wasn't anyone saying, 'Go Mike Go?' and cheering me on to get to Starbucks? I laughed to myself. I went in to order and the girl at the desk said, "Aren't you the guy that pulled a sled?" I smiled and said yes, while I placed my order. The stack of papers had my picture from the day before. I took a copy to read with my tea.

Back at the hotel we started packing up, and getting ready to head for home. This time I'd be in a vehicle. As we drove out of Ottawa on the same roads that I walked in on, tears poured down my face. We got onto the highway and drove even though I was having a very hard time sitting. If you have ever had restless leg syndrome, you'd know the feeling. Now multiply that by a 100 and that's how my legs reacted to sitting. While on route home we had to stop many times due to that. I needed to get out, stretch, walk a bit, stretch and get back in.

Being home felt great, trying to take the stairs didn't. Catching up with my family and getting back into regular routines was overdue and I was more than ready to do both happily. First, I had some phone interviews with radio stations from Windsor. They were follow-ups to interviews I had done before I set out on my journey. Now the questions had changed from, 'How will you do it?' to 'How do you feel now that you've done it?.' I appreciated everyone for taking time out to speak with me.

As I write this, years later, I still reflect and see crystal clear images of the walk in my head. I'm humbled beyond words that I received some national honours, as well as a letter from the Prime Minister's Office. It was incredibly cool to have the opportunity to be the keynote speaker at multiple cancer fundraisers and the Canadian Cancer Society Volunteers dinner. This walk has given me the opportunity to speak at numerous schools where I could connect with kids of all ages. Having them tell me that I've inspired them to want to make a difference are words that I'll never take for granted and never forget. Finding out that some classes at different schools on our route did projects on Help Me Bury Cancer and that classes followed us each day I was on the road was mind-blowing. Meeting and connecting with everyone along the way, could be summed up as priceless. The number one question to me over the years has been, 'Would you do it again?' My answer to that is simple, yes, in a heartbeat.

To use Help Me Bury Cancer terminology, my mom has 'unhooked' her own cancer, and has been in remission since 2013. It was a brutal challenge for her, but she kept putting one foot in front of the other, until she was fortunate enough to come out the other side. We recognize that not everyone can. She reports that it took her years to be able to put cancer to the back of her mind, and knows that black cloud of fear that many patients feel, even after their journey is over. She works at keeping cancer awareness alive through her writing, which she says has been a godsend to her. Her life changed forever because of cancer, including leaving her with a permanent disability, but she is always quick to point out, she feels 'blessed.' Through her cancer journey, she had five young grandchildren, all under 10 years of age. She has lived to see the oldest go off to university, and is thrilled she was here to welcome Erin's and my daughter to the family, three years ago. I asked her if she had any advice to cancer patients, and her answer didn't surprise me. 'Be kind to yourself, and keep putting one foot in front of the other.'

About the Author

Mike is a proud member of the Halton Regional Police Service and is the recipient of various awards in Community Support and Support Services. As a cancer fundraiser, he received multiple national honours, including the Sovereign's and Queens Diamond Jubilee medals.

Mike is a loving husband and father who lives in a small town in Ontario, Canada.

Manufactured by Amazon.ca
Bolton, ON